Second Edition
(Revised and Enlarged)

Your **GUIDE** to

Investment trading

With special
reference to
Singapore and
Malaysia

By
**RODNEY
KING**

CONDITIONS OF SALE

*The publisher and author accept no responsibility
for any loss sustained by any person whose
investment decisions were influenced
by material in this book.*

DEDICATION

This book is dedicated to my father,
Herb King, who laboured long and hard to make
an honest buck on 1700 acres of red dirt,
200 miles east of Perth in the 10-inch rainfall area,
where the salmon gums grow.

ACKNOWLEDGMENTS

*I would like to thank the following people for
their help with this book. They are:
Dr Lau Sie Ting, lecturer at the Nanyang Business School
in the Nanyang Technological University;
Charles Sng and Mark Lee,
of the Singapore Monetary Exchange Limited;
the staff of the Marketing and Membership Department of the
Singapore Commodity Exchange Limited;
Chong Kok Keong, of the Singapore Trade Development Board;
the staff of the Communications Department
of the Kuala Lumpur Stock Exchange;
Benjamin Foo, General Manager and Director
of Phillip Futures Pte Ltd and Phillip Trading Pte Ltd;
and Andrew Szonyi, of Perth Commodities
and Futures Brokers Pty Ltd.
Finally, I owe a special debt to my good friends Stephen Beck,
Luke Fogarty and Ian Kerr and my sister
Glenys Kennedy for editing and proof reading the final drafts.
But any mistakes, omissions or other defects,
are of course my own.*

Cartoons by Ming

PREFACE TO SECOND EDITION

Because change is endemic to today's investment markets books about them date quickly, including this one. In Singapore and Malaysia, several important developments have occurred in the investment field. Among these have been changes to Singapore's CPF investment scheme and the full implementation of scripless trading in Malaysia as well as the continued rapid growth of unit trusts in both countries.

This second edition of Your Guide to Investment Trading describes the latest developments in Singapore and Malaysia's investment markets. It also gives a more comprehensive coverage of Malaysia's investment industry.

I would like to thank the following for their help with the second edition of this book — Ronald Chong, Assistant Manager, (Public Affairs), Central Provident Fund Board; Ms Rusma binti Ibrahim, Deputy General Manager II, Employees Provident Fund, Malaysia; Ms Guri Dhillon, Assistant Manager, Communications and Moorthi Navamani, Junior Communications Officer of the Kuala Lumpur Stock Exchange; Jacob Thomas, Executive Director of the Federation of Malaysian Unit Trust Managers; Bill Belchere, First Vice-President and Head of Fixed Income Research at Merrill Lynch in Singapore, Peter Douglas, Director of, and Corinne Cheok, Business Manager of Aberdeen Asset Management Asia Ltd (formerly Abtrust Fund Managers Ltd). I would also like to thank the public relations and communications staff of the Kuala Lumpur Commodities Exchange, the Malaysian Monetary Exchange and the Kuala Lumpur Futures and Options Exchange for their help.

Contents

General Introduction

Trading in the investment markets is not for the faint-hearted. But for those who like to take calculated risks it can be a consuming pastime. Whether buying shares, selling rubber futures or backing the US dollar to rise against the yen, you are in a game where prospects of sudden wealth compete with the constant threat of impoverishment. Greed and fear will be constant companions, but a cool head and good timing will keep these demons in check.

Certainly, the imagery of the investment markets is not conducive to calm and rational calculation. The common impressions are of dealers milling around on the floor of exchanges yelling prices and signalling to each other or ranks of harassed dealers in dealing rooms staring fixedly into blinking computer screens at rows of figures. But beneath this seeming chaos the immutable laws of supply and demand are determining the price of everything from rubber to Ringgits, soya beans to Swiss Francs, sugar to stock index futures.

Even so, before you start trading you need to understand investment markets, their rules and procedures. You must understood them before you can begin to be an effective player. Knowledge is strength and is critical when playing the investment markets, which can handsomely reward the wise and diligent and ruthlessly punish the ignorant or careless, something that growing numbers of Singaporeans and Malaysians are finding every day. Many have stuck to the share market but others have started trading in the forex, commodities, gold and in the futures and options markets.

Some have prospered. Others would have done better if they had first learnt the basics of investment and trading in the markets. This book is for the novice investor who wants to understand the markets, trading procedures, forecasting strategies and trading tactics before risking hard-earned cash.

Investment success depends first on devising a trading strategy, which means considering the following:

♦ What type of investor you are
♦ Investments best suited to you
♦ Forecasting methods for choosing your investments
♦ Trading tactics.

Investor Type

Investor profile is determined by the amount of money, time and ability you can bring to the task of investing.

First, how much money do you have to trade (invest/play/gamble) with and to risk?

Trading capital significantly limits the markets open to you. Trading in futures, for example, may require $50,000 or more to perform effectively, whereas in shares you can start with a couple of thousand dollars or less.

Second, successful investing usually goes hand in hand with the study and analysis of vast amounts of data. You need to know if you have the time, energy and ability to do this properly.

Third, your emotional make-up will determine the types of investment that suit you. Do you like to take risks and have a gambling streak in you? Or are you the cautious, risk-aversive type who would think twice before buying a lottery ticket?

Types of Investment

Deciding what type of investor you are and your risk tolerance will indicate whether low, medium or high-risk investments best suit you. This in turn will dictate your investment market parameters. Low-risk investments include fixed-interest securities such as bonds, debentures and other types of loan stock. Then there are stocks ranging from safe blue-chip scrips to those for speculative gold and mining ventures.

The most speculative investments are in the "spot" and "derivatives" markets for foreign currencies, interest rates, stock exchange indexes, commodities and precious metals such as gold. You have to decide whether safe securities or speculative spot and derivatives investments are for you.

Section One of this book describes the main investment markets. The first three chapters deal with shares and other securities, the next two look at financial instruments (currencies, interest rates and stock exchange indexes), then we examine gold and commodities, while the final chapters in the section cover the derivatives markets (futures and options).

Forecasting Methods

Whatever the investment, you face the challenge of picking winners from the vast range of prospects and products on offer, whether they be shares, currencies, commodities, etc. Many forecasting systems are available. The main ones (which include technical and fundamental analysis, the Efficient Market Hypothesis and Contrarian approaches) are described in Section Two. The section concludes with an integrated forecasting approach that combines many of the best elements of each system.

Trading Tactics

While a forecasting strategy should help you decide what to buy before it rises and sell before it falls, trading tactics aim to perform both functions efficiently. Market timing (picking the best times to buy and sell), calculating risk-reward ratios and management of investment capital are central to trading tactics. But their effective implementation requires an understanding of the mechanics of trading, the effect of emotions such as greed, fear and hope on investors' judgement and the many other pitfalls which await the unwary.

These topics are covered in Section Three. But to begin — a tour of the investment markets.

1

The Markets

A market is a place where buyers, wishing to exchange money, goods or services for profit or gain, are in contact with sellers who want to exchange goods and services for profit or gain. Thus a market's defining feature is the interaction of the forces of supply and demand. It is not necessarily confined to some specific geographical location. Buyers and sellers can be brought together by a complex network of telecommunications, banks, broking houses or other financial institutions.

Investment markets trade assets which can range from extremely short-term (speculative) to long-term investments. In economic terms an asset itself is anything that has a monetary value — i.e. can be exchanged for money. But for an asset to have investment potential it needs to possess certain qualities. First, it must be a store of value. This means it must be durable. A tonne of bananas has monetary value. But they do not keep long so they will not be useful as an investment unless of course they can be traded in the form of a futures contract as will be explained later.

Second, an investment asset should be able to increase in value over time, or at least produce some sort of steady income for its owner, preferably both. Many assets can do this. The most common is the family home, the biggest investment asset that most people will acquire in their lives. Not only is it durable, but it usually increases in value over time. Also, when rented, a house can produce income.

Other investment assets range from antiques, jewellery, even to Edwardian teddy bears (some of which reach values of $20,000 or more). But such investments are unlikely to yield income and are not very liquid — they are difficult to buy and sell quickly. Thus, a third requirement of an investment asset is that it should be as liquid as possible. The more liquid an asset the greater its investment value.

Some people invest in Edwardian teddy bears.

Shares have always scored high on all three counts. The companies they represent are durable entities (more or less); shares can greatly increase in value, and they normally yield income in the form of dividends. Other popular investments have been interest-bearing investments such as bonds (liquid investments that provide security and yield regular income) and gold. While the latter does not produce income, it is extremely durable, highly liquid and capable of dramatic increases (or decreases) in value.

More recently the commodities and foreign currency markets have provided a wide range of investment opportunities for investors — usually of a short-term speculative nature. Though commodities markets exist to trade agricultural products and raw materials, and the currency markets to provide foreign exchange for commercial and trade purposes, they have both acquired an investment function over the decades. Again, liquidity and endless opportunities for capital appreciation/depreciation provided by commodities and forex markets are the main reasons.

Today the main investment trading markets are the markets for securities (shares and interest-bearing stock such as bonds), foreign exchange, commodities and gold.

But investment markets themselves are also classified in several other ways, depending on whether such assets are traded:

- ◆ Through exchanges or by the more informal trading networks of Over-the-Counter (OTC) markets, and
- ◆ As derivatives (mainly futures and options) or on the spot (or cash) markets.

Exchange-based and OTC Markets

Exchange Markets

Much investment trading has been done through established regulatory bodies such as exchanges. Of these the oldest have been exchanges for trading in shares and commodities. More recently, exchanges have been established for trading such financial assets as currencies and interest rates. When traded as futures they are transacted through futures exchanges.

Exchange trading is conducted through exchanges that are regulated by rules and by-laws, usually instituted with the approval of the government, to control membership requirements and conduct, and to protect investors. For example, the Stock Exchange of Singapore (SES) operates under the approval of the Finance Minister and its members pay into a special fidelity fund that assures the financial protection of the investing public against any default by an SES member.

Besides the SES, Singapore's other exchanges are the Singapore International Monetary Exchange (SIMEX) and the Singapore Commodities Exchange (SICOM). SIMEX trades in spot forex and futures and options forex (foreign exchange) contracts as well as crude oil and fuel oil, gold, bonds and stock market indexes. SICOM trades in rubber and coffee futures.

In Malaysia there are four exchanges. The best known is the Kuala Lumpur Stock Exchange (KLSE). The others are the Kuala Lumpur Commodities Exchange (KLCE), its subsidiary the

Malaysian Monetary Exchange (MME) and the Kuala Lumpur Options and Financial Futures Exchange (KLOFFE).

Finally, there are many exchanges in other countries that Singapore and Malaysian investment markets constantly deal with. Apart from major stock exchanges and money markets these include: the Chicago Board of Trade (CBOT) and the Chicago Mercantile Exchange (CME) and the London Loco (gold and silver).

OTC Markets

Essentially OTC markets are conducted outside established exchanges and are dominated by banks and brokers who are linked together by a telecommunications network. Also, the assets traded are not so standardised as those traded on exchanges but are tailored to suit the risk profiles and specific requirements of customers.

OTC markets were originally for trading shares of smaller companies that did not meet exchange regulations. Also, they were sold to the public by brokers who worked outside stock exchanges. But now OTC markets are used to trade almost any product including currencies, company shares, commodities, gold and a wide range of derivatives.

Many bucket shops that trade in commodities operate like bookmakers.

There are two levels to the OTC network in Singapore and Malaysia. The first consists of regulated banks and registered members of such bodies as SIMEX, SICOM and the KLCE who provide a safe and reputable trading network for investors. The second level consists of unregulated companies and operators. Among these are the notorious "bucket shops" who solicit orders from clients but do not execute them on any recognised exchange with legitimate counter-parties. They are somewhat similar to illegal bookmakers who bet against their clients where they stand to gain from their clients' losses.

Because the bulk of their revenue comes from commissions, these bucket shops "churn" their clients accounts by entering trades (most of which are unauthorised by their clients) as often as they can. Bucket shop clients have little protection and at the time of writing Singapore authorities had already removed bucket shop operations from local forex trading.

Spot and Derivatives Markets

Investment markets can also be classed in terms of whether they are of the spot or derivatives variety.

Spot Markets

The terms "cash", "actuals" or "physicals" are often used synonymously with spot markets. You buy something for cash and then take possession of it. More generally though, spot market transactions see ownership transferred from seller to buyer with delivery of the asset immediately or soon after. The buyer assumes ownership while the seller relinquishes it, whether the items traded are durians, diamonds or investment assets such as shares or commodities.

In the investment world the importance of the spot market is that an asset can be purchased at its current market (or spot) price, rather than of some price in the future as is the case with derivatives.

Usually the term "spot market" is used in relation to forex, commodity or gold trading, though in theory it can be applied to any markets which trade assets on a cash basis.

Derivatives Markets

The future is the key variable in the derivatives markets. Whether in the form of forward contracts, futures (standardised forward contracts) or options contracts, players are buying or selling obligations and rights to deliver, or receive delivery of, an investment asset at some future date. The price you pay will be for the asset on that date. That will be the price you will have to pay then. Even so, this future price will subsequently continue to fluctuate with market perceptions of what its value should be right up to that date.

Again, while spot market transactions involve transfers of present ownership of an asset, derivatives involve a transfer of future ownership. How futures and options contracts work will be fully explained in Chapters Eight and Nine. But as they will often be referred to before then, a brief description of them will now follow.

Futures Contracts

Every futures contract has a buyer and a seller — a party who buys the contract and another who sells it. Buyers agree to take delivery of the contract's asset within a specified period (usually three months), while sellers agree to deliver the asset at that time.

Those who BUY a contract have taken a LONG position in the market. They are bullish because they believe the contract's asset (called the underlying asset) will rise. Conversely, those who SELL the contract have taken a SHORT position in the market. They are bearish, believing the asset's market price will fall.

The basic principle of buying a futures contract is like

buying something with a deposit and then agreeing to take possession of it at some future date, when theoretically the balance is due. For example, Lee has agreed to buy Tan's car for $100,000 in one month's time. Tan has agreed to hand it over (or deliver it, to use futures parlance). If, during that time, the market value for that car has dropped to $90,000, Lee must still pay $100,000 for it and Tan has made $10,000 more than he could reasonably expect to make based on current market values.

Again, should the car's value rise to $120,000 during that month, then Tan must still sell it to Lee for $100,000. Lee of course could then immediately sell it for $120,000 and make $20,000 on the deal.

To use futures parlance Lee has taken a long position, believing the value of the car would rise, and as such has agreed to buy it for $100,000 in one month. Conversely, Tan has taken a short position, believing that the car's value will fall, and so has tied Lee into buying it at $100,000 before the price fall. In such a situation a "bull" car market will favour Lee and a "bear" car market would profit Tan.

However, if there were a futures markets dealing in contracts to buy and sell cars, the speculators would move in. The contracts would be bought and sold between parties depending on whether they thought the market would rise or fall. Moreover, most of the time (as occurs in real futures markets) no car would be delivered. Also, contracts would be "closed out" before delivery between the parties. Here the losing parties (those who the market had moved against) would pay in cash what they had lost to the winning parties (those the market had favoured). Under such an arrangement, Lee would have had to pay Tan $10,000 if the price of the car had fallen by $10,000 to $90,000 during the 30-day term of the contract. Conversely, Tan would have had to pay Lee $20,000 if the car's price had risen by $20,000 to $120,000 during the contract period.

In addition, if this was a real futures market, the Lees and Tans trading in it would rarely meet each other. Second, they could deliver, or request delivery of the car at any time within the 30 days from when the contract was initiated. Third, the contracts they were trading between each other would be handled by a futures exchange via brokers, who would represent clients who were parties to the contracts. The contracts would be constantly changing hands over the 30 days between buyers and sellers as the price for the contracts continually fluctuated. Fourth, a series of the contracts would be for assets that were standardised in terms of quality, quantity, price and delivery terms. In other words, every car traded would be exactly the same. Chapter Eight will explain this process further.

Options

While futures contracts involve obligations to deliver or take delivery of a specified asset, options involve merely the RIGHT to do this. The holder of an option has the right to buy or sell a given asset up to a specified price at a designated date. A fee, called a premium, is paid by anyone who wishes to exercise such a right. Most often options are used in the share, forex and gold markets. Options are further described in Chapter Nine.

The investment markets trade in a wide variety of investments in many complicated ways, either through regularised exchanges or informal OTC networks and on either a spot or derivatives basis. They often trade the same type of investments, though in different ways. How they do this will be the main focus of this section, which will describe the main investment assets traded and what factors affect them.

CHAPTER ONE

Shares and Other Securities

*T*he capital markets have always been a magnet for those need-ing funds for some dream or scheme. The entrepreneur with the brilliant idea, but no money; the conman whose only aim is to fleece the gullible one day and disappear the next; the blue chip company that needs capital to pay for some major new project; or the free-spending government borrowing from the public to meet its latest budget deficit, have all been capital market players. Over the centuries they have all found that the capital markets (usually called the share or stock markets) give them unparalled access to people's savings.

Capital markets exist so that those who need to raise money can make contact with those who have surplus funds. Since the 18th century these markets have set up such bodies as stock exchanges to facilitate their activities.

Stock exchanges trade in investment assets called securities, which are of two basic types:

- ◆ Shares, which involve owning part of (having equity in) a company
- ◆ Loans at fixed rates of interest to companies or governments.

Unfortunately, terms for both types of investment are often confused. For example, both shares and stocks can describe equity investments in the UK, Singapore and Malaysia. But the word stocks (in the UK and here) can also mean fixed interest loans, often called bonds or loan stocks.

To further confuse matters shares (equities) are termed stocks in the US and fixed-interest investments (often called stocks here) are always known as bonds there. Finally, the exchanges which trade in both shares and bonds are called "stock exchanges". Aiyoh!

In this book shares will mean equities in companies, while stocks will be used interchangeably with loans or bonds (i.e. fixed interest investments). The terms "share market" or "stock market" will be synonyms for the securities market, where both equities and loan stocks are traded.

Thus investors who buy shares have a stake in a company — a piece of the action. If the company prospers so do they; if not they can lose much if not all of their investment.

Stockholders however provide loans to government or private enterprises as fixed-interest investments. Interest is paid at regular intervals on the loans, which are repaid in full at maturity. Stocks carry much less risk than shares and should the company fail they will be paid before shareholders. But if the company prospers, stockholders will still receive the same interest, while shareholders will get higher dividends.

However, stockholders can often convert their stock into shares in a company or be given warrants with the stock they acquire entitling them to buy shares at discounted prices.

We have described just two of the many hybrid forms that securities can take. The many other types will be outlined later. But first we should take a brief look at the history of stock exchanges, including those of Singapore and Malaysia.

Historical Background

Stock exchanges have been defined as organised markets for dealing in the securities of business and government. They are the best known and oldest of the investment markets.

Their origins are found in 18th century London. People seeking to raise capital would meet with would-be investors in coffee shops where shares in business ventures were traded, dividends paid and reports made on ventures in progress. Eventually the formation of the British Stock Exchange in 1773 replaced these informal coffee house exchanges.

"WANT A PIECE OF MARKET ACTION DEARIE..."

GREAT SOUTH SEA TRADING COMPANY

SALT WATER INTO GOLD VENTURE

England's first stock markets operated from London coffee shops during the 18th century.

Singapore's share market began in an equally informal way in the late 19th Century in a little room in the Arcade, where Clifford Centre now stands. Equities traded were stakes in British rubber and tin companies in Peninsular Malaysia. Unorganised share trading continued at a low level until the 1910 rubber boom when stock markets quickly burst into prominence.

However, following the 1929 Wall Street crash, 15 stockbroking firms formed the Singapore Stockbrokers Association in June 1930 to regularise the industry.

By the late 1930s stockbroking had rapidly grown in Peninsular Malaysia and so, in 1938, the Association was reconstituted to include stockbroking firms from across the causeway and renamed the Malayan Stockbrokers Association. Even so, for the next two decades, trading was still conducted between brokers and clients without a proper trading room. In March 1960, 10 Singapore and nine Malaysian firms established the Malayan Stock Exchange to provide proper trading rooms and shares were traded publicly with share prices shown on a board. Two trading rooms were set up, one in Kuala Lumpur and the other in Singapore. In 1962 they were linked by direct telephone lines.

The exchange was renamed the Stock Exchange of Malaysia in 1964, after Malaysia gained independence. When Singapore left the Malaysian Federation in August 1965 the exchange was named the Stock Exchange of Singapore and Malaysia.

However, in May 1973, when the Malaysian Government decided to end the currency interchangeability arrangement between the Malaysian ringgit and the Singapore dollar each country established its own exchange. The new exchanges were named the Stock Exchange of Singapore (SES) and the Kuala Lumpur Stock Exchange (KLSE). Though the Malaysian and Singapore stock exchanges were separate entities, they co-listed about 60 per cent of their 300 plus counters.

The SES

Following its establishment in 1973, the SES has aimed to make Singapore a major financial centre, which would not only serve the Republic but also the region and beyond. To this end the SES has expanded and diversified its operations. Apart from its main board, which consists of established local companies, the SES has established two more trading boards — SESDAQ and Clob International — and has also set up a NASDAQ link with US markets.

SESDAQ

In recent years stock exchanges have "second-tier" stockmarkets, established to help smaller, but promising companies raise public money for their continued growth. Many such companies are in the high technology areas or in the health and sports, entertainment or real estate sectors. Lack of capital has often curbed their growth. For them the listing requirements of many exchanges are too strict, usually met by only well-established companies with large resources. To deal with this problem and help smaller concerns, second-board markets with easier listing requirements were created.

London's second-tier stock market is the Unlisted Securities Market (USM), has been operating for some years. In February 1987 the SES launched the Stock Exchange of Singapore Dealing and Automated Quotation System (SESDAQ) for smaller companies and one year later the KLSE did the same with its Second Board.

In time the more successful second-level companies can apply for listing on the main board. But mighty oaks from little acorns do not always grow. Some SESDAQ companies will fall by the wayside and their investors lose money. But high-risks can also mean high-rewards. Carefully chosen SESDAQ stocks can yield high profits.

CLOB International

The third board of the Singapore stock market, CLOB International (named after the Central Limit Order Book trading system), was introduced in January 1990 after the KLSE delisted 160 Malaysian-incorporated companies from the SES. To permit Singaporean investors to continue trade in Malaysian shares the SES introduced CLOB, an OTC market operation. Later this arrangement was subsequently extended to Hongkong, Indonesian, Philippine and European companies.

CLOB companies are not officially listed on the SES, like the Main Board or on SESDAQ. As such they are not subject to local listing requirements and the SES's corporate disclosure policy. Even so, CLOB companies have been carefully screened and are governed by a set of trading rules.

NASDAQ

In March 1988, the SES further broadened international investment opportunities. It created a fourth securities market where Singaporeans could trade in selected US stocks. SES linked up with the National Association of Securities Dealers (NASD) in the US to provide quotations and other trading information on 25 companies traded on NASDAQ (The National Association of Securities Dealers Automated Quotation System). This way Singaporeans can trade in high-technology stocks listed on the US OTC market. The companies include Apple Computer, Intel, Microsoft Corporation, Ericsson and Volvo and the Indonesian company, Tri Polyta.

Data transmitted daily between the US and Singapore at the close of each country's markets includes the best bid and offer quotes, the last transactions and trading volumes. Prices are in US dollars.

However, at the time of writing, NASDAQ was experiencing a difficult period. Growing numbers of NASDAQ dealers were quitting the market because stricter rules and other factors had cut their profits. With fewer dealers to trade their stocks, many companies that traded on the market had also left it. Stocks traded on NASDAQ have dropped from 450 to 150.

The KLSE

Following its formation in 1973 the KLSE has taken a series of steps to create a modern, efficient and well-developed bourse. The KLSE sees its central role as attracting and mobilising local and foreign capital for national development.

Milestones in the KLSE's growth include:

- ◆ Computerisation of the clearing system in 1984 with the formation of a central clearing house – the Securities Clearing Automated Network Services Sdn Bhd (SCANS).
- ◆ Introduction (1986) of the KLSE Composite Index, which is now the market's main barometer.
- ◆ Launching of the KLSE Second Board (1988) for small company listings.
- ◆ Implementation of the SCORE (System on Computerised

Order Routing and Execution) which did away with the open outcry system in 1989. But this system was only a semi–automated trading system as matching remained manual. Only in October 1992 was fully automated trading (both order and entry matching) implemented.

♦ Introduction of scripless trading through launching of the Central Depository System (CDS) in November 1992 to produce a more efficient settlement and clearing system. By the end of 1993 all Second Board counters were in the CDS and by early 1997 so were all Main Board counters, making the KLSE fully scripless.

♦ Implementation of the WinSCORE system (broker front-end trading system) in 1994 which gives each dealer a single integrated work station for credit control management, order and trade routing and confirmation.

These improvements by the KLSE have accompanied significant developments in Malaysia's securities industry as a whole including:

♦ Replacement of the Securities and Industries Act (SIA) of 1973 with a new SIA in 1983 to provide better supervision and control of the industry.

♦ Establishment of a Securities Commission in March 1993 to oversee the industry's sound development.

Such advances have done much to make the KLSE the largest bourse, by market capitalisation, (M$747.61 billion) in ASEAN and the fourth biggest in Asia. By April 1997, there were 639 listed companies on the KLSE of which 220 were Second Board counters.

Primary and Secondary Markets

The first purpose of any capital market is to raise equity or loan capital for both the public and private sectors. Normally capital is raised in a primary market for securities which are then traded in a secondary market — the stock exchange. Shares can be floated in a primary market through a limited liability company and then be listed and traded on the exchange. In the same way companies can also float bond and loan issues. But in Singapore few corporate bond issues are raised compared with share issues.

Gaining public listing has several advantages for a company. Raising capital will enable it to better finance its daily operations and to expand in many ways. For example, the capital from the extraordinary shares can be used to acquire other companies, increase resources or facilities and can also give it greater capacity to hire the best professional staff.

Professor Tan Chwee Huat in "Financial Markets and Institutions in Singapore" has described several ways companies issue new securities before they are traded on the stock exchange.

Public Issues

One of the commonest ways companies float a new issue is by making a direct offer to the public. They do this by distributing a prospectus with an application form inviting people to subscribe for the securities being offered at a specified price. This method is used for both share and loan/bond issues.

Normally companies appoint an underwriter who will guarantee that the issue is fully subscribed in return for an underwriting commission. Underwriters — usually banks, merchant banks or broking firms — are required to ensure that all the shares are taken up at the stated price.

Offers For Sale

These come from the underwriters or other issuers of securities which have been floated for a company. As part of their obligation such parties have to buy any securities which have not been taken up by the public or institutions. They will then offer them to the public later. This practice is not so common in Singapore.

Private Placements

These involves issuing securities to selected buyers. The company may arrange for a bank or broking firm to buy the issue and on-sell the securities to clients.

Bonus Issues

Extra shares are offered free by a company to existing shareholders, depending on how many of the company's shares they already have. For example, one new share may be given to share holders at no extra cost, for every three shares held.

Bonus issues are simply an accounting exercise whereby assets the company has accumulated since its last share issue are converted into extra shares. As a purely paper operation it adds nothing to the company's total assets. Shareholders have paid nothing for the new shares and their proportionate ownership of the company remains the same. While they may have more shares, the total value of their shares remains the same. The only difference is that the company simply issues more shares to existing share-holders.

Rights Issue

With rights issues existing shareholders get the preferential right to subscribe for new shares being issued by a company. The new shares are usually issued at below their current market price. Shareholders can exercise their rights to fully or partly accept the offer or reject it outright — the decision depends on the market value of the share.

Like bonus issues, rights are offered to shareholders on a proportional basis. But, unlike bonus issues, a rights issue increases the company's wealth because new money is injected into the company. If you do not wish to take up a rights issue you can sell your rights allotment in the market before they fall due — usually at a discount. Sometimes it might even be cheaper to buy in the market than exercise a right.

While these are the main ways that companies raise capital on the stock exchange, they also do this through a variety of securities.

Types of Securities

The main types of securities traded on stock markets are shares (equities), interest-bearing securities (both government and corporate), convertibles, warrants and unit trusts.

Shares

These are the best known securities. The two main types are ordinary and preference.

Ordinary

As the term suggests shares mean you have a share (or equity) in a company upon which you will be paid a variable interest rate called a dividend, depending on the company's fortunes. If the company does well, dividends will be high; if badly, no dividends may be paid.

A share is defined by the Penguin Dictionary of Economics as "... one of a number of equal portions in the nominal capital of a company entitling the owner to a proportion of distributed profits and of residual value if the company goes into liquidation". In other words shareholders get what is left of net profits after debts, interest and corporate taxes have been paid. And, if the company goes bankrupt, shareholders get a bit of whatever remains after the company's other creditors have been paid.

Preference

Shares of this type are not so common in Singapore and Malaysia. Their holders get preference over those with ordinary shares in payment of interest or dividends. Also, should the company fail, any left-over monies after debts have been paid, will be paid out to preference shareholders before ordinary shareholders (but after debentures holders, as will be explained below).

Against this, preference shareholders get only a fixed dividend rate, payable only if the company earns sufficient profits. Also, they do not benefit from rising dividends if the company does well. They cannot vote at general meetings, nor have a say in the selection of company officers or directors.

Preference shares are of two types — non-cumulative and cumulative. The difference between the two becomes apparent when a company has had a bad year and preference share-holders fail to receive a dividend. Any unpaid fixed dividends for cumulative shareholders will be carried over till such time as the company makes a profit. This is not the case for non-cumulative share-holders. A dividend missed is gone forever.

Interest-bearing Securities

A wide range of interest-bearing securities, usually at fixed interest rates, are traded on investment markets. At one end there are the government bonds and corporate bonds and debentures in reputable companies. At the other end are high-risk loans stock with negligible asset backing — "Junk Bonds" (and all they imply). Naturally, the interest such securities pay reflects the degree of risk they carry for investors. The greater the risk, the higher the interest rate.

Singapore's domestic bond market is still thin and poorly traded, both government and corporate. Because government, government-linked companies and the bigger corporations possess huge cash reserves they do not need to raise money through bonds. They can finance expansion with internal funds, share issues and bank loans.

Malaysia's local bond market however has been developing

rapidly since the 1970s, largely due to government borrowings to finance its development program – and since the late 1980s by strong government support for corporate bonds. Total bonds issued grew from M$3.5 billion in 1970 to M$74.1 billion by the end of 1994.

Generally, most interest-bearing securities traded on world money markets are fixed-interest. But some securities, such as floating note rates, have variable interest rates. Even so all such securities fall into two main categories – government or corporate.

◆ Government

Government bonds and treasury bills are generally regarded as the safest securities of all because they are backed by a government guarantee. Both are financial instruments used by the government to borrow money from the public.

A bond carries a fixed rate of interest, usually payable quarterly, half-yearly or annually with the principal redeemed after a fixed time. Bonds are usually medium to long-term investments, whereas treasury bills are short-term. If there is a secondary market for bonds they can be sold at any time before maturity for cash.

In Singapore, the Monetary Authority of Singapore (MAS) auctions bonds quarterly and treasury bills weekly. Treasury bills have maturities of 91 days, 182 days or 364 days and are issued in minimum denominations of $10,000. Bonds are issued in $1000 denominations with maturities of two to five years.

In 1994, only $3.8 billion in Singapore government bonds were issued. And 82 per cent of these were merely replacing $3.1 billion issued the previous year.

In Malaysia, Bank Negara Malaysia (the central bank) auctions 91-day, 182-day and 364-day Malaysian Treasury Bills (MTBs) on a weekly biweekly and monthly basis respectively.

Minimum denominations are M$1000. Medium and long-term government bonds range from two to 21 years, with the bulk of them having a maturity of 11 years or more. Denominations are also M$1000.

Despite the growth of Malaysia's bond market the government's share has been shrinking since the late 1980s because of frugal fiscal and debt policies. As a result the annual issue of government bonds fell from M$7.4 billion in 1988 to M$2.5 billion in 1994.

◆ *Corporate*

The interest-bearing securities issued by companies are also often referred to as corporate bonds. They reflect varying degrees of risk, depending on whether they are secured or unsecured with least secured paying the highest interest rate.

The most secure non-government securities are usually debentures — loans secured by particular assets, such as property, capital equipment or on liquid assets (stocks or trade debtors). The company guarantees debenture holders will be paid a fixed interest on specified dates, regardless of whether a profit is made. Moreover, should the company default and fail to pay interest the debenture holders have a right to put in a receiver to run the business, or liquidate the company or take whatever action they deem necessary to protect their business and investment.

For unsecured loan stocks there is no mortgage or asset backing. Should the company wind up, the unsecured stock will rank after the secured stock. But both rank before the company's ordinary shareholders. Again, in Singapore, low interest rates encourage local companies to raise capital through bank loans other than bond issues. In 1994, Singapore-incorporated companies raised only $5.4 billion through the stock market. One of the largest corporate bond issues in recent years was one for $200 million made by Parkway Holdings to help fund its purchase Tenet Healthcare Corp's Asian health-care operations. In recent years the view has been expressed that Singapore's underdeveloped bond market has been an obstacle to the Republic becoming the region's major capital and financing centre. The Singapore Government has moved to encourage statutory boards and government-linked companies to tap capital markets rather than rely on local banks and other customary sources of finance.

While there has been a big drop in the issue of government bonds in Malaysia, the slack has been taken up by the private sector since the corporate bond market was launched in 1987 with the establishment of Cagamas Berhad (the National Mortgage Corporation). Cagamas repackages housing mortgages into debt instruments and trades them in the inter-bank market providing liquidity to banks. Corporate bonds issued grew from M$1.8 billion in 1988 to M$8.4 billion by 1994.

Convertibles

Preference shares and loan stocks are termed convertibles when they can be exchanged for a company's shares on given dates at a fixed price. The conversion price is usually fixed throughout the life of the convertibles but can be adjusted before maturity to reflect rights or bonus issues. Convertibles are a popular way for listed companies to raise extra working capital. Investors can enjoy regular interest income and security of principal and possible capital gain, if the shares rise in value above the conversion price. If they do not appreciate, investors need not exercise their right and can cash in the convertibles at maturity date without any capital loss.

Warrants

A warrant or Transferable Subscription Right (TSR) gives the holder the option to subscribe for a given number of a company's ordinary shares at a specified price and within a given period. Though a warrant's life-span is fixed, the purchase (or subscription) price can be adjusted to reflect changes in the market price of the company's shares. Warrants can be converted either on any day during their life span, or only on certain specified dates.

Usually warrants are not issued on their own but are provided free by a company to encourage subscription to its rights or loan stock. Frequently those who have been given warrants detach them from the loan stock and sell them on the markets for an immediate profit.

Warrant=holders can also make capital gains by exercising their warrants and buying underlying ordinary shares at a special discount price (the subscription price), then selling at the normal market price for a profit — provided of course the market price is higher than the subscription price.

Once warrants have been issued by a company they are listed on the market where they can be traded normally. Often they can be cheap alternatives to the company's shares because they usually move in the same direction on the market.

A warrant's value depends on many factors. Two of the most important are the price of its underlying ordinary shares and its subscription price. For example, a company's shares may be trading at $1.20. But the subscription price for its shares if purchased with a warrant may be $1 and the current market price for warrants to buy its shares at that price might be 30 cents. Thus the investor would pay 10 cents more than necessary if he bought the warrants and used them immediately to buy the shares.

Cost of warrant	$0. 30c
Sub cost of share	$1. 0
Total cost of share	$1. 30
Market price of share	$1. 20
Net loss	0.10c

However, an investor may still decide to buy the warrant because he believes that before the expiry date the share's price may rise above $1.20 if he thinks the company has good prospects. Of course he could simply buy the share outright, but would have to pay $1.20, rather than merely 30c for the warrant, a far greater financial outlay. As long as the warrants have not expired and their price goes up he could sell them on the market and make a profit that way.

Unit Trusts

People who want to invest in the share market but are limited by time, money and expertise often find unit trusts appealing. Unit trusts investors pool their money and allow a professional fund manager to invest it. The manager decides where the money should be invested and when profits should be taken.

The professional manager has the time and resources to study the market full time, as well as handle all the administrative work, such as payments connected with share trading, registering shares, col lecting dividends and applying for rights issues.

Fund managers usually buy a portfolio of shares and other securities. The total amount is then split into equal units and offered for sale. Each unit, often for amounts of $500 (but some-times as low as $100), has a fraction of each security bought. You need only one unit to invest in a unit trust and the fund manager must buy back the units from you whenever you want to sell. But being open-ended funds, there is no limit to the number of units available. New units can be created or cancelled depending on the demand.

Unit trusts spread risk. A fall in one sector such as industrials or hotels will often be balanced by rises in other major sectors. Moreover, being mainly composed of blue chip stocks, the market value of unit trusts tend to fall more slowly than the overall market during bearish times and rise more slowly during boom periods.

Unit trust dividends are distributed to unit holders either six-monthly or yearly. Units-holders can be individuals, companies or institutions, who invest funds to gain income in the form of dividends, interest and capital gains.

The rights of unit-holders are protected by company law. The assets of a unit trust are held by an independent trustee on behalf of all the investors. The trustee acts as a watchdog to protect unit-holders' interests. In Singapore the Registrar of Companies is the authority which approves trust deeds for establishing unit trusts.

In recent years unit trusts have surged in popularity and total funds managed by them soared from $430 million in 1991 to $2.39 billion by mid-1996 in Singapore. By May 1997 there were 62 unit trusts available to Singaporeans. Of these 14 were based on Singapore securities; 13 on Singapore/Malaysian securities, and 15 on regional markets. A further 10 were country-specific unit trust funds for securities traded in such countries as Japan, the US, China and India while the remaining funds were specific to investments in property and infrastructure (3), gold (2) or global bonds (5).

(The Directory of Personal Investment 1997, published by Financial Planner gives a comprehensive descriptions of all the above unit trusts available in Singapore).

In Malaysia too unit trusts have taken off and are becoming a major part of its investment industry. The Malaysian Investment Fund, which was established by Asia Unit Trusts Berhad in December 1966, was the country's first unit trust.

By mid-1995 there were over 50 unit trusts in Malaysia and these had grown to 94 by April 1997.

(Investing in Unit Trusts in Malaysia by Sally Cheong gives a comprehensive coverage of Malaysian unit trusts till late 1994).

◆ *Growth Funds*

They aim for high capital gains and invest in stocks with strong growth potential, but minimal dividend payments. Such funds are best for investors with above-average risk tolerance.

◆ *Income Funds*

A healthy income stream is the aim of such funds, rather than capital gains, and are usually bond-based. They have a lower risk factor and are designed for those who want financial security.

◆ *Balanced Funds*

These are a mixture of the above two and focus on blue chip shares and high-grade bonds.

◆ *Sector Funds*

Investments are restricted to a particular industry sector such as property.

CPF and EPF Approved Funds

These are unit trusts that have been approved by the CPF in Singapore and the EPF (Employees Provident Fund) in Malaysia for investment by their members.

Previously investment of CPF assets was dictated by the Basic Investment Scheme (BIS) or the Enhanced Investment Scheme (EIS). But from January 1 1997 they were merged to form the CPF Investment Scheme (CPFIS) to give CPF members more options for investing their CPF savings while providing financial security after retirement.

Meanwhile, in Malaysia, first steps have been taken towards allowing EPF members to invest some of their savings in approved unit trusts.

Chapter Three will describe both schemes further.

Unit trusts make securities investing simple, but at a price. The major cost members pay to join a fund is called the loading. This usually consists of the sales charge(called the front-end load) and sometimes an exit fee. Other costs are management fees and administrative charges.

The sales charge covers advertising and promotion costs incurred in marketing the fund. In Singapore, this usually ranges between 3 and 5 per cent of the amount you invest with a fund, with 5 per cent as the norm. But the front-end load for bond funds can be as low as one per cent. There are also funds with no front-end fee, mainly in the US. But one such fund in Singapore is the Keppel Enhanced Fund.

The front-end load is basically the difference between the buying and selling price of the fund - i.e. the bid-offer spread, which is normally 5 to 5 1/2 per cent in Singapore. For example, a fund might be selling its units for $2 (the offer price) and buying them back for $1.90c (the bid price). The 10c difference or the 5 per cent spread becomes the front-end load that you pay for investing in the fund.

More precisely though the front-end load is calculated on the basis of the Net Asset Value (NAV). The NAV is the current market value of the fund's total investment portfolio (including dividends due from securities in that portfolio) less fund expenses, divided by the total number of fund units. When people buy into the fund they are charged a fee, which is a percentage of the NAV (usually 5 per cent). Thus they pay for the fund's units at the prevailing NAV plus the fee (i.e. its offer price). When an investor sells, the fund simply pays out its current NAV (the bid price).

Apart from the front-end load, other costs are:
- Management fees range from 0.5% to 1.5%. The more complex and exotic the fund, the higher such fees are likely to be.
- Administration charges to pay for such items as stamp duty and

trustee, custodian and registrar fees which range from 0.2 to 0.5 per cent.

♦ Sometimes an exit fee that has to be paid when an investor sells his units - usually about 1 per cent when levied in Singapore. But to compensate the fund may reduce its front-end load by that amount.

In Malaysia, the fee structure is similar, though management and trustee fees are based on Gross Asset Value (GAV) rather than the NAV. As the term implies the GAV is the total value of the fund's portfolio of investments, before any deductions. The GAV in Malaysian unit trusts can be up to 20 per cent higher than their NAV, meaning that GAV-based fees can also be that much higher. The three main fees levied by Malaysian unit trusts are:

a) A front-end load of 5 to 7 per cent when you join a unit trust, based on the fund's NAV as in Singapore. Here too the front-end load can be calculated from the difference between the bid-offer spread. Check a fund's prospectus to see what their load is. New regulations implemented in May 1997 require unit trusts to publish the load in their prospectuses.

b) A annual management fee averaging about 0.5 per cent a year, based on the fund's GAV when the fee is levied.

c) Annual trustee fees which average 0.08 per cent and are also GAV-based.

Securities by Sector

Not only are securities classified by whether they are equities or interest-bearing investments, but also by what economic sector they belong to. Securities traded on the SES fall into the following categories:

♦ Industrial and Commercial
♦ Finance
♦ Hotel
♦ Properties

◆ Plantations

At present nearly 250 companies are listed on the SES's main board and 46 on SESDAQ. In addition, 233 bonds, loans and warrants from various companies are traded on the SES.

But what factors move the prices of shares and other securities? The next chapter will look at this.

References

"Directory of Personal Investment 1997" *by Financial Planner*
"Financial Markets and Institutions in Singapore" *by Tan Chwee Huat*
"Handbook for Stock Investors" *by Goh Kheng Chuan*
"How to Invest in Stocks and Shares" *by Robert Chia and Doreen Soh*
"Investment Management" *by Saw Swee-Hock*
"Investing in Stocks and Shares" *by (Catherine) Tay Swee Kian*
"Investing in Unit Trusts in Malaysia" *by Sally Cheong*

CHAPTER TWO

What Moves Share Prices

*F*our groups of factors determine the supply and demand and hence the prices of shares and other securities.

- Macro factors such as the state of the economy, inflation and interest rates as well as political events and government policies.
- Industry factors that affect all companies in a particular sector of the economy.
- Micro factors affecting individual companies
- Market mood and emotion (to be discussed in Section Two)

Macro Factors

Main macro-economic factors that affect the share market are:

- GDP growth rates
- Inflation
- Interest rates
- Political factors
- Liquidity

GDP Growth Rates

It is always assumed an economy's growth rates have a profound affect on the share market. Certainly economic booms tend to have a positive effect on the market, while recessions usually do the opposite. At the same time the securities market reflects the fortunes of listed companies; when their profits and prospects improve during boom times their share prices will appreciate. The converse is often true, with share prices sliding during recessions, when corporate profits are down.

But the correlation between the state of the economy and the share market is imperfect at best. For example, for the period 1950-90, the Standard and Poor's 500 stock index in the US moved in the same direction as the GDP in 25 out of 41 years — 61 per cent of the time. However, if you had adopted the simple-minded strategy of betting that the S&P would rise every single year during that period you would have been right 83 per cent of the time. Again, during the 1950-90 period there were four years in which an above-average rise in the US's real GNP was accompanied by an absolute decline in share prices.

In fact, the evidence suggests that share markets lead rather than follow the economy. A comparison between each year's GDP growth rate and the S&P 500 index for the preceding year produced a match in 36 out of 41 years, which is an 88 per cent rate.

One of the most dramatic demonstrations of this theory was provided by the 1929 Wall Street crash, which not only preceded, but was instrumental in triggering off the Great Depression of 1929-33. A more recent example was the continuation of the bull market in the US despite the 1990-1 recession, when low growth rates and high unemployment prevailed. At that time, some US share market commentators described the market's upward trend as "defying the law of gravity".

In recent years the US stock market seemed to be defying the law of gravity with its constantly rising prices.

Inflation

Some market analysts maintain inflation is the key to understanding the share market. Certainly, prospects of rising inflation is one of the biggest factors likely to dampen the share market.

What share prices reflect most is what investors think companies will earn in the future. When the economy is expected to grow, share prices will rise. When the economy is expected to slow, share prices will fall.

Expectations about inflation will significantly dictate investors' expectations about company prospects. Companies are harmed by inflation because it cuts into their earnings. Hence, when inflation looms, the smart investors sell up. They know that with falling corporate profits share prices are likely to soon start falling.

However, when inflation is low, and not likely to take off for a while, prospects for business growth are good. Economic growth can rise from say 1 to 4 per cent without igniting inflation. Shares will respond to that growth potential by rising sharply, often long before the economy shows signs of real growth. During the 1990-1 recession US shares rose 20 per cent between January and April, but the economy only started to recover in May-June of 1991.

COMMODITY PRICES

The most common way to measure inflation has been through CPI (Consumer Price Index) measures. But changes in commodities' costs are central to inflation. "They're the basic building blocks of all that's produced — the fuels, metals, paper, and grains and other foodstuffs that are refined, grounded, pounded, and packaged into life's luxuries and necessities," notes US investment analyst Stephen Leeb. Commodity price rises push up the cost of most other products and services in a chain reaction.

However, with the possible exception of oil, price rises for a single commodity have little impact on shares and stocks. They have to move up more or less as a group to significantly affect inflation. Wall Street's most popular index for measuring commodity prices is the Commodity Research Bureau's (CRB) futures index. This is a composite index for 21 commodities, from pork bellies to orange juice.

Even so, the CRB index is for future prices and includes some commodities that have only a marginal effect on the economy. Another CRB index that has a strong and proven effect on the economy, consists of these commodities:

Burlap

Copper scrap

Cotton

Hides, heavy native

Lead scrap, heavy soft

Print cloth

Rosin, window glass

Rubber, No 1 ribbed
  smoked sheets

Steel scrap, No 1

Tallow, prime

Tin, grade A

Wool tops (nominal)

Zinc, prime western

Lead time for this index is 12 months, and if it has dropped over the previous year, then the share market should expect a good year. If the index has risen significantly during this time, then a bear market looms.

Interest Rates

For Leeb and others interest rates are seen as having little, if any effect on securities markets. They regard interest rates as largely a reflection of inflation, though higher interest rates can occur during periods of low inflation. At such times their driving force is not inflation but high growth, which has created demand for investment funds, forcing interest rates up. From 1948-65 US stocks rose 500 per cent, but short-term interest rates rose from 1 per cent to 4 per cent and inflation averaged only 1.7 per cent. Here interest rates did not reflect inflation.

Again, most share market players are strongly affected by interest rates fluctuations, whether or not they reflect inflation. For this reason every interest rate move by central banks, such as the Federal Reserve in the US ("the Fed"), the Bank of England or the MAS is closely watched by the market. As Leeb notes: "...it's not uncommon for the market to head up or down 50 points or more in response to slight shifts, or even the hint of a shift in the Fed's interest rate policy."

Falling interest rates make shares more attractive, while rising rates do the opposite. When interest rates on bonds and similar securities rise, investors tend to put their money into these financial instruments rather than shares. But when interest rates fall the opposite occurs and money flows back into the share market and share prices rise. Hence a share market is bearish when there are rumours the government will raise interest rates and bullish when interest rates cuts are looming.

Political Factors

When considering political factors one needs to look at both the domestic and the international situation.

Countries such as Singapore with a stable political environment and sound laws to protect investors will always have a much stronger share market than countries which lack these conditions. Political instability and frequent changes of government adversely affect share markets. Again, government policies pertaining to foreign investment, and monetary and fiscal matters, especially those relating to interest rates, capital inflows and outflows and taxation, can also significantly impact markets.

International crises have also profoundly affected share markets. For example, Iraq's invasion of Kuwait in August1990 caused dramatic falls in share prices around the world. In Singapore the Straits Times Industrial Index plunged from 1557 to 1127. Such events create uncertainty among investors and make them want to get out of the shares and into gold, or some other asset they perceive as a safe haven for their money.

Liquidity

The availability of investment funds is heavily determined by interest rates. But many other factors, both domestic and foreign, can also affect the level of funds available for the share market.

Singapore has seen a big upsurge in share market liquidity through the liberalisation of rules for use of CPF funds in recent years. With more money available for investment the local share market has been more buoyant than would otherwise have been the case.

However, inflows and outflows of foreign capital are also assuming increasing importance for share markets around the world, including Singapore's. In the Asia–Pacific region foreign capital did much to fuel renewed bullish share markets in Singapore and Malaysia in 1995 and early 1996. The persistently high growth rates of these countries – combined with the foreign perception that they have the most developed and sophisticated stock exchanges in the ASEAN region – has attracted a growing volume of foreign capital to their share markets.

Industry Factors

Besides considering general market conditions, investors in shares and other securities must also determine which segments of the market are performing best. In any economy some industries are performing better than others.

Concentrating on industries that are doing well will save investors a lot of time in making share selections by helping them to more easily locate companies with good prospects.

A promising company in an industry with poor prospects will be severely handicapped compared to an average company in a sector with high-growth potential. Moreover, when a specific industry is performing well most of the share prices of companies in that sector will rise.

One of the most dramatic demonstrations of this occurred during the nickel boom in Western Australia during the late 1960s. The prices of mining companies with the most flimsy of prospects (little more than a few unproven leases and a couple of holes in the ground) experienced enormous price leaps. The whole mining sector was booming. In more recent years hi-tech and biotechnology stocks have generated similar investor excitement.

Conversely, industries in decline will pull down the prices of promising companies in their sector. At various times construction, mining, shipping and the retail sectors have gone through down periods. At the time of writing, the retail sector in Singapore had been in recession for several years.

Stock exchanges facilitate industry analysis by classifying listed companies into broad categories. As indicated earlier, these are industrial and commercial, finance, hotel, property and plantation on the SES. However, the industrial and commercial sector are too big for industry analysis. Sub-dividing them into food and beverage, retail, trading and shipping and construction would greatly help investors make selections.

When doing sector analysis investors should also keep in mind industry life-cycles. The four main phases are regarded as: pioneering, growth phase, rapid expansion phase and maturity (and often eventual decline). You need to determine the stage an industry is at to accurately assess its growth potential and prospects.

Micro Factors

Selecting individual companies involves looking at such factors as competitive position, industry and economic conditions, financial strength, expansion plans, accounting policies and the record of sales, earnings and dividends. Such factors are both tangible and intangible, financial and non-financial.

FINANCIAL

Sales, profits, borrowings, working capital and assets are major financial indicators of a company's health. Many have been expressed in a series of ratios and measures commonly used for investment analysis. Together they can give investors an overall picture of a company's financial strengths and weaknesses.

We will begin by looking at the terms dividend, dividend yield and earnings per share, then at the financial ratios based on them.

The Dividend

The amount of a company's net profit that is paid on each issued share of that company to shareholders is the dividend. For example, the XYZ company which has issued 10 million shares and paid a total of $2 million in dividends to shareholders will have a dividend of 20c per share.

Dividend Yield (DY)

The DY is calculated by dividing the **current** market value of a company's shares by its dividend. Thus if XYZ's shares were trading at $2.40 and their dividend were 20c then percent-age-wise its DY would be 8.5 per cent.

Earnings Per Share (EPS)

This is one of the most widely used measures of a company's performance. The EPS is calculated by dividing the TOTAL amount earned by a company by its number of ordinary shares. The EPS expresses the company's earnings per share rather than the dividends shareholders will receive.

For example, if the XYZ company earns a total of $4 million after tax (of which $2 million has gone to shareholders as dividends) on its 10 million shares then its EPS is 40 per cent.

However, companies usually "gross up" their dividends by including the corporate tax paid on the dividends. Thus if they paid 33 per cent corporate tax, then their pre-tax profit would be one-third more at $6 million, giving the XYZ company a "grossed up" EPS of 60 per cent.

Dividend Payout Ratio (DPR)

The DPR derives from the proportion of profits the company will pay shareholders. Some companies will want to keep the bulk of their profits for expansion and pay only a small percentage to shareholders. They may prefer to plough back profits into promising ventures which will produce greater long-term earnings.

Other companies though, will adopt a generous payout policy producing higher dividends to make their shares more attractive to investors. They are termed income companies and attract investors more interested in dividends.

Debt/Equity Ratio (DER)

The DER is to determine how much debt the company has compared with its equity (the book value of shareholders' funds). The higher the ratio, the larger the company's debt burden and the greater investment risk it represents. A high ratio means the company will have to generate high earnings to service the debt. If revenues slump the company could face liquidation.

Price-Earnings Ratio

This is the best-known of all the financial ratios used in company analysis. In fact it often dominates the thinking of investment experts when assessing company prospects. The PE-ratio is obtained by dividing the market price of the share by the earnings per share. For example, if the XYZ company's shares are trading at $2.40 and its EPS is 40 per cent then the PE-ratio is calculated as:

$$\text{PE-ratio} \quad = \quad \frac{\text{Market Price of Share}}{\text{Earnings Per Share}}$$

$$= \quad \frac{2.40}{0.40} \quad = 6$$

The PE-ratio is of course only applicable when a company is making a profit and cannot be computed when it is taking losses. In the above example the company's shares are said to be selling at six times earnings. In other words it would take six years for earnings to reach the shares' current market price.

The higher a company's earnings, the lower its PE-ratio. Companies with low PEs are those which have been neglected by the market. Astute professionals often believe such companies have the greatest profit potential, while offering far less risk than their more popular brethren with higher PEs. For them a low PE-ratio suggests the company's earning power is strong and it is currently undervalued. But, when they and other smart investors realise this, more of the company's shares will be bought and its price will rise. But so will its PE ratio unless dividends keep pace with its rise in price. Eventually the share could be bid to such heights that the ratio between its price and earnings will become much greater and its PE will rise dramatically.

The PEs of "hot stocks" can soar to unrealistic heights. For example, in early 1961 IBM was seen as the wave of the future, having enormous potential. As a result, by late 1961 IBM's price had rocketed and its PE-ratio had hit 70 — three times that of the average S&P 400 stock. Investors' enthusiasm had lost touch with reality. There was no way IBM could justify such hopes and as a result its shares fell by more than half in 1962. Again, during the Malaysian bull market of 1993, PE ratios were pushed to the 37-40 range.

Thus while high PEs reflect high market hopes for some investors, for others they indicate low profits and poor prospects.

When is a share's PE too high? This depends on:

◆ The share's PE compared to the market average
◆ The current inflation level.

One major US study has shown that over long periods shares with low PEs dramatically out-perform those with high PEs. This was demonstrated by shares on the New York Stock Exchange for a 26-year period from 1959 to 1984. The study showed that shares in the lowest 20 per cent in terms of PEs generated the highest return (15.8 per cent a year), while those in the top 20 per cent returned only 6.4 per cent a year. (Returns were dividends plus capital gains). The following table illustrates the returns for each quintile (20 per cent segment) of the companies' PEs studied.

Quintile		Return
Lowest 20%	–	15.8%
Second "	–	11.7%
Third "	–	9.8%
Fourth "	–	7.0%
Highest "	–	6.4%

There are a couple of qualifications you need to remember before rushing out to buy low PE shares. These are:

◆ Low PE shares in some industries can languish for years, even decades.
◆ PE-ratios for cyclical shares can be deceptive. For example, the auto, steel, savings and loans, construction and securities industries often go through pronounced cycles. When business is booming the profits of companies in these industries are huge and PE ratios are pushed down. You

have to be sure such low PE ratios do not reflect a boom time which has finished.

Investors are likely to improve their prospects with low PEs shares if they also consider the current inflation environment. If inflation is high then seemingly low PEs compared to the market average may still be too high. As already pointed out, share markets have usually run out of steam by the time high inflation is present. Buying any shares in a runaway bull market with inflation looming is unwise, even if the share has a low PE relative to the market.

But during times of low inflation, when the market is starting to gather momentum, even above-average PEs can still offer good growth prospects.

Note: PE ratios for Singapore and Malaysian companies are listed in the financial pages of the daily newspapers.

Other Financial Indicators

Along with these ratios other financial indicators of a company's performance should be examined to get a more complete picture of its prospects. They include:

◆ *Sales:* Are they falling or rising? Most failing companies experience falling sales. This can be due to many factors, including a declining product cycle and competition from rival firms. Conversely, rising sales indicate growing demand for a company's products. This can be due to increased market share or because the company has a new product in the market before its rivals.

◆ *Profits:* Profitability is an obvious indication of a company's health, both in the short-term and when reflected in more long-term measures such as PE ratios. Growing profits may show expanding markets, greater efficiency, better cost-cutting measures or the development of new and popular products. Declining profits — and more especially losses — can indicate a falling market share, reduced efficiency and out-dated or unappealing products as well as poor sales generally.

◆ *Working Capital:* How much capital a company has will significantly determine its capacity to expand and capture new business opportunities. Profitability again is a key factor. Rising profits will boost working capital, giving the company greater resources to draw on. Declining profits will reduce working capital, limiting capacity for expansion. But reductions in working capital can also be due to heavy debt servicing requirements because of high borrowings.

◆ *Borrowings:* Though a healthy company may borrow to exploit new business opportunities, loans can also be used by a failing company to mask its financial problems. It may be trying to maintain the required level of working capital by borrowing instead of tackling declining profits due to falling sales and profitability. Also, more debt can cut profits further through extra interest payments.

Over-borrowing occurs for many reasons, including lack of control over CEOs. Companies dominated by ambitious autocrats, because of weak finance directors, can get more loan money than they should. This will cause the ratio between borrowed money and shareholders' equity to fall, requiring a growing percentage of the company's profits to be spent on debt servicing.

Financial indicators, together with the financial ratios described earlier, can be useful guidelines to a company's health and prospects. But they need to be interpreted against the backdrop of prevailing economic and inflationary conditions. On a company level they need to be assessed in the light of a number of non-financial factors, which can also reveal much about a company's prospects.

NON-FINANCIAL

Though harder to pin-down and estimate the following non-financial factors profoundly affect a company's health.

◆ Management quality
◆ Efficiency of accountancy systems
◆ Responsiveness to change.
◆ Growth rates
◆ Expansion projects

Management Quality

This factor depends on:

◆ *Degree of Vision* — A management must have definite ideas on what the company's image should be, how to market its products and/or services and must identify selling points to potential buyers and plans for expansion and growth. Managements that do not display these traits lack vision, resulting in poor planning and ad-hoc responses to challenges and problems.

◆ *Degree of All-round Business Skills* — Managerial ability and the skills required to efficiently run a company's production, administration or marketing operations are also critical to corporate success. Poor management has sent many promising companies to the bottom.

One particularly important managerial ability is resourcefulness, the capacity to make maximum use of a company's resources. Misuse and waste of resources are signs of an out-of-control management and a company in decline.

Poor management has sent many promising companies to the bottom.

Accounting Systems

Companies need accurate and comprehensive accounting systems to keep track of revenue and expenditure. Poor accounting systems often fail to do this. They can also fail to bill customers promptly and systematically. Accounts may be paid slowly, harming cash flow, or not at all, harming profitability.

Again, a slack accounting system may cause slow payment of bills by the company, damaging its reputation and credit-worthiness. In addition, accounting systems should be not only efficient but also honest. Signs of "creative accounting" in corporate reports and balance sheets should ring alarm bells for investors. "Cooking the books" clearly indicates something is wrong and the company may even be resorting to fraud to hide problems. Such accounting occurs most often when financial information has to be reported to external parties. It can be characterised by excessive depreciation of assets and the presence of extraordinary items and expenses, not normally found in company balance sheets.

Responsiveness to Change

In a world of ever-faster change, the capacity to positively respond to new trends and challenges is critical to business survival. Successful concerns can respond positively to change. Those that can not have failed.

Poor adaptability is shown by such traits as out-of-date production facilities and products. The management may also display outmoded attitudes to employees and a lack of the latest skills, including computer literacy. Yet again the board of directors may be old-fashioned and out-of-touch with market and industry trends.

◆ *Expansion* — Rapid expansion can be a two-edged sword. While building new plants, acquiring larger premises and generally upgrading production capacity may show a vibrant and expanding operation companies can also over-reach themselves with "The Big Project".

Undertaking a project beyond its resources can severely damage or even bankrupt a company.

The project can be the launching of a major new product or marketing programme, or the establishment of a subsidiary which runs into financial problems and must be bailed out. For example, the State Bank of Victoria in Australia failed because one of its subsidiaries became bankrupt. Eventually the State Bank had to be taken over by the Commonwealth Bank of Australia.

In addition, there are other specific indicators of a company's health, which can either point to trouble ahead or that things are ticking over nicely. They can either give rise to reasons for concern or optimism about a company's prospects.

Reasons for Concern
◆ Management salaries being frozen
◆ Capital expenditure decisions being delayed

- Product quality or service deteriorating
- Market share falling
- The chief executive being ill
- Staff turnover rising and low morale
- Rumours abounding that the company is in trouble
- Dividends not being cut when they should be

Reasons to be Reassured
- Management salaries are rising with little opposition from shareholders
- Capital expenditure decisions are being fast-tracked to meet rapid expansion plans
- Product quality and service is improving
- Market share is increasing
- Chief executives are energetic and apparently healthy
- Staff turnover is low and morale appears good
- Dividends are rising

These are the macro and micro-economic factors, both general and specific, financial and non-financial, which affect the share market and the prices of individual issues. But, to thoroughly assess these factors, you need to have adequate information about them.

Sources of Information

Knowledge is strength, and nowhere is this more true than with the investment markets. Ignorant investors are gambling when they trade. Apart from good knowledge about the state of the economy, inflation and interest rates, share market investors require detailed information on specific companies. They first need to be aware of the types of shares and other securities available in the market. Also they should know:

- The daily performance of shares and the operation of both macro and micro factors affecting their value
- When bonus and rights issues will be made

- When dividends are declared and paid
- When a company is planning a new venture
- When take-over bids are made
- Changes to a company's top management and board memberships

These are the minimum types of information that investors require if they are to make intelligent investment decisions. Sources for such information are numerous and diverse.

Current information about particular shares, as well as about the share-market generally, can be obtained in the many newspapers, magazine and journals and newsletters available to Singapore and Malaysian investors. The most obvious of course are the local daily newspapers, The Straits Times and Business Times and the New Straits Times. Basic information given by the Straits Times includes:

- Daily prices of all shares and other securities traded on the SES, as well as on the KLSE and the Tokyo and Hongkong stock exchanges.
- Total daily volume traded
- Number of counters which rose and fell
- Major price changes for the day.

(A comprehensive account on how to read the Straits Times Money pages can be found in "How to Invest in Stocks and Shares" by Robert Chia and Doreen Soh).

Apart from the daily newspapers and business magazines published in Singapore and Malaysia, a whole range of publications are available from the SES. Among these are:

- Daily Financial News — a complete record of the day's trading
- Weekly Financial News — announcements and news from listed companies
- Company Statex Service — provides investors with the latest financial statements on companies
- SES Journal — a comprehensive monthly report on the Singapore stock market, which includes a statistical summary for every trading security.
- Annual Fact Book — mainly statistical data about the Singapore

stock market.

- ◆ Annual Companies Handbook — provides basic information on every company listed on the SES.

The KLSE also provides a wide range of publications describing daily, weekly and monthly prices and market conditions on the Malaysian securities market.

Annual Reports

However, in-depth information about specific companies can usually be obtained only by a close reading of company reports and financial statements. Only then can many of the financial ratios as well as sales, profits, borrowings and working capital be calculated. Also, through such reports an investor can get a "feel" for the non-financial variables affecting the company's performance — such as the quality of the management, the company's accounting systems and future expansion plans. The following procedure should be adopted when reading company reports.

Start With the Auditor's Report

When reading company reports it is best to begin with the auditor's report. The auditor is an independent accountant legally responsible for approving the annual accounts and statements and telling investors whether they conform with accepted accounting principles. One phrase to watch out for is "subject to". Here the accountant is saying that some item in the report is only acceptable if you take the company's word for it. This is a hint from the accountant that perhaps you should not.

Furthermore, if "subject tos" are accompanied by a change in auditors the company may be trying to hide something. A frequent change of auditors indicates a search for "compliant" auditors prepared to obscure corporate shenanigans.

Read the Footnotes

In company reports, a lot of detailed chicanery can sometimes be buried in the footnotes. Normally footnotes are meant to qualify some statement or claim that would otherwise make the company's prospects glow. Good company news will be set in large type, bad news in miniscule type. The following items should be looked for in the footnotes:

♦ Revaluation of company assets such as land and buildings to boost company book values.

♦ Earnings boosted by one-off sales of company assets, which will not be repeated the next year.

♦ Mark-downs of company merchandise and other stock (inventories) which indicate the company is stuck with outmoded or unsaleable stock.

♦ Expansion plans, requiring heavy expenditure that may strain the company's financial resources.

♦ Higher materials costs that could cut profits.

The Chairman's Statement

For those who can read between the lines the Chairman's Statement can be quite revealing. Significant omissions should be noted, especially those relating to the company's trading record or other key activities for the year. The chairman may choose instead to talk about the quality of company management, or market conditions likely to favour the company in future. And when he mentions the future does he foreshadow major changes for the company? Is it getting into more new areas than it can handle and ones which it has little knowledge of?

Also, watch for qualifications such as "Notwithstanding", "Even so", "Except for" or "Despite the...". Such phases can be used to obscure real problems the company is facing.

Financial Statements

The two most important items contained in a company's annual report are its balance sheet and profit and loss statement.

The Balance Sheet

This describes assets, liabilities and company capital and reserves as they stood on a particular day, such as December 31 or June 30.

◆ *Assets*

These are either fixed or current.

Fixed Assets — either tangible (land, buildings, plant, machinery and vehicles, office equipment and furniture and fittings), intangible (goodwill) or investments (quoted shares).

Current Assets — stock, trade debtors, short-term bank loans and cash.

◆ *Liabilities*

Bank overdrafts, trade creditors, current taxation and dividends payable.

◆ *Capital and Reserves*

Share capital, share premium, retained profits and short-term loans are classified as capital.

Share capital consists of paid-up capital subscribed by share-holders.

The share premium is the excess value of shares over their par value and is classed as capital reserve.

Retained profit is the share of profits the company decides to keep.

Reserves include the excess of current over book value of land and buildings arising from revaluations.

Profit and Loss Statement

While the balance sheet gives a snapshot of the company on a given day, the profit and loss statement summarises the company's operations over the past financial year. This describes total revenue flowing in and out of the company during a 12-month period.

From the detailed data contained in the profit and loss statement one can see revenue sources and the expenses incurred by the company.

Also, one can calculate the various financial ratios, described earlier.

Note: Detailed though they are, figures published in company annual reports are normally about six months out of date. The economic climate generally, as well as individual companies' fortunes, can change dramatically in that time.

Useful References

"Contrary Investing for the 90^s" *by Richard E. Band*
"Financial Markets and Institutions in Singapore" *by Tan Chwee Huat*
"Handbook for Stock Investors" *by Goh Kheng Chuan*
"How to Invest in Stocks and Shares" *by Robert Chia and Doreen Soh*
"Investment Management" *by Saw Swee-Hock*
"Investing in Stocks and Shares" *by (Catherine) Tay Swee Kian*
"Market Timing for the Nineties" *by Stephen Leeb*

CHAPTER THREE

Securities Trading in Singapore and Malaysia

G one are the days when trading at the SES and KLSE was performed through the noisy open outcry method. Now all trading is fully computerised, using the CLOB system in Singapore and the KLSE's SCORE-computerised trading system. Computer trading terminals, located in the offices of stock exchange member companies, are linked to the exchange's central computer system.

$2·50! $1·70! $15·30! $3·50!

The days of open outcry on the SES and KLSE are gone.

When an SES broker receives an order to buy or sell from his client he enters it into the CLOB through his trading terminal. CLOB records the order then matches buy and sell orders and confirms the transactions. Orders that are not matched by the close of the trading day will automatically lapse.

At the end of the trading day all transactions are transferred to each stockbroking firm's computer system. The firm then sends out contract notes to clients to confirm that transactions have been completed.

The KLSE's computerised trading system consists of two major computer systems – SCORE and WinSCORE. SCORE is the exchange's central computer engine for matching orders while the WinSCORE work stations at stockbroking companies handle credit control management, order and trade routing and confirmation.

Orders are entered directly by dealers into WinSCORE work stations at stockbroking companies for each trading session. Unexecuted orders at the end of each session must be re-entered into the system for execution.

During the first 30 minutes of each trading session order queue sequence is determined by the central SCORE computer system using a randomised algorithm. Orders entered after that period are dealt with on a first come, first served basis.

Matching of orders is by price and time preference, but market orders have priority over limit orders. Once the orders are matched and confirmed the information is relayed electronically to stockbroker companies.

Both CLOB and the KLSE's computer system are seen as superior to the open outcry system for several reasons. First, where there are similar orders trade execution is strictly according to time priority, based on the sequence in which they were entered into each system. Second, orders are matched according to price priority so investors are more certain of getting the best possible prices than with the more rough and ready open outcry method. Third, orders are executed more quickly because they are processed by computers, rather than by hand. Fourth, the greater efficiency of both systems and their speed in processing orders can generate much higher turnovers and greater liquidity for the market, making it easier for traders to enter and exit the market more quickly.

Another major development in Singapore and Malaysian share

trading have been the introduction of scripless trading, loosening of restrictions on CPF investment and initial steps by the EPF to permit some investment of funds by its members and, in Singapore's case, the introduction of the ASSETS system.

Scripless Trading

The introduction of scripless trading by the SES and KLSE has made share trading a high-tech business on both exchanges.

A central computer at each exchange links all market participants and records all transactions. Share certificates no longer have to be delivered between buyer and seller because every transaction is a book entry and no scrip changes hands. All investors receive is a statement of account recording their trades. Needless to say, scripless trading has greatly reduced the backroom workload for both the exchange and stockbroking firms.

Central to scripless trading on both exchanges are central depository account systems.

In Singapore the Central Depository account system (CDP) was set up in early 1987 to permit investors to trade and settle transactions on a scripless basis. First used for SESDAQ stocks, the system was then extended to the Main Board in May 1990 and by July 1995 all SES-listed Singapore stocks were being traded on a scripless basis.

Central Depository (Pte) Ltd is a wholly owned subsidiary of SES which serves as a custodian for shares and other securities traded on the SES. The CDP acts as a central nominee with all securities deposited with it registered in its name. The CDP merely holds the securities for owners. It has no rights to them.

The CDP provides Automated Self-Service Enquiry Terminals (ASSETS) to allow investors to inquire about the CDP, securities balances and new share allotments. On request ASSETS can print a statement of your share portfolio and issue a confirmation statement of your shareholdings. ASSETS terminals can be found at CDP and in SES member stockbroking firms.

The KLSE move to scripless trading began in November 1992 when the Central Depository System (CDS) was launched. The first counter was put on the system in March 1993. By the end of 1993, all Second Board counters were on the CDS and by early 1997 all Main Board counters.

Singapore's CPF Investment Scheme

There was a time when Singaporeans' Central Provident Fund (CPF) savings were meant to be used only for housing, medical care and old age. Not till 1978 did the Singapore Government permit CPF savings to be used for buying shares, but limited to only Singapore Bus Services (SBS) shares. In May 1986, under the Approved Investments Scheme (AIS), CPF members were given greater flexibility to manage their CPF savings.

The BIS and EIS-amendments in October 1993 mean there are two schemes whereby CPF account-holders could invest part of their CPF savings in shares, loan stocks, unit trusts and gold – the Basic Investment Scheme (BIS) and the Enhanced Investment Scheme (EIS)

Under the BIS, CPF members were permitted – from April 1, 1994 – to invest up to 80 per cent of their CPF balances above the then $35,400 minimum sum in their Ordinary or Special Accounts, whichever was lower. The BIS allowed investments in Main Board trustee shares on the SES, approved convertible loan stocks and unit trusts and 10 per cent in gold or SES non-trustee shares.

Under the EIS, CPF members could invest up to 80 per cent of their CPF balances above the $50,000 minimum in their Ordinary and Special Accounts on either the Main Board or SESDAQ. The EIS permitted a broader range of investments than the BIS, including: approved non-trustee shares, government bonds, Singapore fixed-dollar deposits, endowment insurance policies and fund management accounts.

The above two schemes were merged into the CPFIS on January 1 1997. This freed more funds for investment and increased CPF members' investment choices.

Under this scheme, 80 per cent of CPF funds can be invested after setting aside the Minimum Sum which currently stands at $45,000. But this 80 per cent can not be more the balance in the Ordinary Account after a cash component of $8000 has been set aside from the cash total of both accounts.

For non-Singaporeans who are unfamiliar with the CPF scheme the following account may clarify things a bit.

Deductions from employees' incomes are paid into three types of accounts - Ordinary, Special and Medisave. But only the first two concern us here. The amounts paid into each account depend on the person's age. But most gets paid into the Ordinary account and a small proportion into the Special Account for CPF contributors up to age 55. Moreover, money can be withdrawn from the Ordinary account under the various CPF schemes for such purposes as buying a house or paying for education.

But how is each contributor's investible amount calculated? Read on.

Mr Wong has $54,500 in his Ordinary account and $3000 in his Special account and has withdrawn $38,500 from his Ordinary account to buy a house. How much therefore does he have to invest?

MR WONG'S ORDINARY ACCOUNT		HIS SPECIAL ACCOUNT	
Total paid in	$54,500	Total paid in	$3000
Amount withdrawn for house	$38,500		
Cash balance in Ord. A/C	$16,000		

Thus Mr Wong's total CPF savings are $57,500 ($54,000 plus $3000).

From this is deducted $45,000 (his Minimum Savings)to give him $12,500 (his Investible Savings). He is allowed to invest 80 per cent of this $12,500, giving him an Available Withdrawal Limit (AWL) of $10,000.

But he can only invest this $10,000 if it is less than the Cash Component of his total CPF savings. To see whether or not this is so we do the following calculations:

Cash balance in Ord A/C	$16,000
Cash component of that must be kept in the 2 accounts less the $3000 already in the Special Account	$8000
	$5000 (net cash component)
Ordinary account balance less net cash component	$11,000

Here Mr Wong's AWL of $10,000 is less than the $11,000 cash balance in his Ordinary Account. So under the CPF rules he has $10,000 to invest. If his AWL had been $12,000, then the Ordinary account balance of $11,000 would have been made available instead for him to invest. Moreover, the Minimum Sum will increase every year by $5000, from July 1 1997 until the sum reaches $80,000 a year by 2003. Also, the cash component will be increased by $4000 annually until 2000 and then by $5000 a year after that.

The following investments are permitted under the CPFIS:
- ♦ Full paid ordinary and preference trustee and non-trustee shares and loan stocks of Singapore incorporated companies listed on the Mainboard and SESDAQ of the SES. However, only 20 per cent of the investible amount (or sub limit) can be invested in non-trustee shares and loan stocks.

- Approved loan stocks.
- Gold (up to 10 per cent of the sub-limit)
- Government bonds
- Bank deposits
- Unit trusts
- Fund management accounts
- Endowment insurance policies

CPFIS investors can keep capital gains and dividends from the investments in excess of what the invested amount would have earned in interest with the CPF. If losses occur investors do not need to make up the losses at once. However, when they enter the market the next time and make profits the losses will be offset from the profits. Only then can surplus capital gains and dividends be withdrawn.

Before participating in the CPFIS members must open a CPF investment account with an approved agent bank. At the time of writing the following were approved agents banks:

- Development Bank of Singapore Ltd
- Industrial and Commercial Bank Ltd
- Keppel Bank of Singapore Ltd
- Overseas-Chinese Banking Corporation Ltd
- Overseas Union Bank Ltd
- Tat Lee Bank Ltd
- United Overseas Bank Ltd

Malaysia's Employees Provident Fund (EPF)

In November 1996, an investment scheme for EPF members was launched in Malaysia. The scheme allows contributors with more than M$55,000 in Account 1 to withdraw 20 per cent of the excess from their EPF accounts for investment in approved unit trusts. To date there are 29 approved trusts. By April 1997 a total of 12,968 members (out of a total of 139,400 eligible) were participating in the scheme.

Many in Malaysia's unit industry believe that this is only the first step to liberalise the EPF for investment purposes.

Useful References

"Directory of Personal Investment 1997" *by Financial Planner*

"Financial Markets and Institutions in Singapore" *by Tan Chwee Huat*

"Handbook for Stock Investors" *by Goh Kheng Chuan*

"How to Invest in Stocks and Shares" *by Robert Chia and Doreen Soh*

"Investment Management" *by Saw Swee-Hock*

"Investing in Stocks and Shares" *by (Catherine) Tay Swee Kian*

CHAPTER FOUR

Foreign Exchange

F oreign exchange plays a crucial role in the global economy. It is the medium through which international trade and commerce are conducted. But unlike stock exchanges, foreign exchange (Forex) markets have no specified physical location. Instead they constitute markets without borders whose participants are linked around the world by complex telecommunications systems.

Trading on these markets determines the exchange rates for each currency. But what are exchange rates? They are the value of one currency in terms of another. The factors that dictate exchange rates will be described later but first a look at the forex markets.

The Forex Markets

Most nations have forex markets for exchanging their own currency for foreign currencies. They form a global network where commercial banks, foreign exchange dealers and brokers bring buyers and sellers of foreign exchange together.

By April 1995, US$839 billion foreign exchange and interest rate derivatives were traded daily on world forex markets. Overall about US$1 trillion are traded on international finance markets. The world's top five forex centres listed in descending order in terms of forex derivatives traded daily are:

1. UK   US$301 billion
2. USA $137
3. Japan $112
4. Singapore $ 63
5. Hong Kong $ 56

Some US$105 billion daily is traded in all financial instruments on Singapore financial markets.

While the US dollar is the dominant currency the other major currencies traded are Japanese yen, German Deutschemarks, British pounds and Swiss francs.

Forex markets operate on two levels — wholesale and retail.

Wholesale Markets

Also called the inter-bank market, wholesale forex markets trade billions in foreign currency daily. Two rates are quoted — the spot rate and the future or forward delivery rates.

In theory the spot rate applies to the immediate delivery of currencies. In reality the spot rate is today's rate of exchange delivered in two days' time. In news about foreign exchange the rates quoted are spot rates.

Forward or futures rates are for foreign currency contracts at times ranging from a few days to one year or more. Though based on the same principle of future delivery there are many differences between futures and forward contracts.

Essentially futures contracts are forward contracts in which all conditions are standardised. They include specifications regarding the amount of the asset to be delivered and duration. Also, the clearing house guarantees performance of futures contracts.

Forward contracts though are tailored to individual customer needs and are traded on the OTC markets, through banks and SIMEX members. Moreover, forward contracts are available only to a limited number of buyers and sellers, usually larger customers with established lines of credit. Public speculation in forward contracts is discouraged.

Those who wish to speculate in forex would trade on the spot market or in futures or options contracts where they have access to margin facilities. In both spot and derivatives forex trading (as in commodities and gold), traders are given enormous leverage to make or lose large sums.

However, futures trading is more formalised, being done through regulated exchanges such as SIMEX, whereas spot trading is conducted on the OTC markets, both reputable (banks and registered broking houses) and the disreputable (bucket shops).

In spot trading you pay the current market price for forex, whereas on the futures market the price you pay is what the market thinks the asset will be worth at some given future date. For example, the spot price for the US dollar on March 14 against the Singapore dollar might be S$1.40, but a US dollar forex contract maturing on May 31 may have a price of S$1.45 because that is what the market thinks the US dollar will rise to against the Singapore currency by that date.

The Retail Markets

In the retail or cash market, banks and money changers buy and sell foreign currencies with the public who exchange their local money for foreign currency with a bank or money-changer. Rates can change with every trade in the wholesale market, but they are fixed for the day in the retail market.

The difference between the two constitutes the bank or money-changer's profit margin. Sometimes the forex retail market is also regarded as a sort of OTC market because customers can buy any amount of currency to suit their requirements.

Other important aspects of forex markets to consider are:

◆ Trading methods
◆ Transaction costs
◆ The players
◆ Round-the-clock trading

Trading Methods

Transactions on the forex markets, as on the other markets, are either performed in futures exchanges or on the OTC market. If through an exchange, futures contracts are traded by open outcry between buyers and sellers on the floor of the exchange or in the newest exchanges through a screen-dealing system. The bid is the price the buyer wants to pay while the offered price, is the seller's price.

However, spot forex and forward contracts are normally traded through the OTC network consisting of banks and brokers. Together they determine the buy and sell prices which, of course, will reflect current market prices.

Transaction Costs

This depends on whether futures, spot or forward contracts are being traded. With futures a commission must be paid, as with other types of futures contracts. But with spot and forward contracts, banks do not charge commissions when buying and selling foreign currencies but rather profit from the spread or difference between the buying and selling rates. For example, at the time of writing Singapore banks were buying US dollars for S$1.3942 and selling them for S$1.3947. The 0.0005 difference between the two prices was the spread and the profit banks made on the transaction. This might seem a miniscule margin but with many thousands of transactions, each involving hundreds of millions of dollars, it all adds up.

Again on the retail market, banks and money-changers also profit on the spread between the wholesale and retail prices.

The Players

Main forex players are multi-nationals, importers and exporters, money brokers, commercial and merchant banks and trading companies managing multi-million dollar portfolios. These players trade in spot, forward/futures forex — either for business, hedging or speculative purposes.

Spot forex is required for such purposes as paying for immediate imports while hedgers use forward or forex futures as a risk management tool. Speculators trade in spot or forex futures to profit from market fluctuations.

Those who trade in forward contracts are mainly hedgers —

mostly companies, especially multi-nationals as well as importers and exporters and others wanting protection from currency fluctuations during their business dealings.

They want to be sure that they can buy or sell a given amount of foreign exchange at some specified future date. However, those interested in speculation confine themselves to spot or forex futures. Thus, while hedgers intend to use or deliver the currency they trade through forward contracts, speculators do not.

Consequently, over 90 per cent of forward contracts are settled by actual delivery against only 3 per cent of futures contracts. Futures contracts are usually closed out before any delivery takes place. In futures trading a close out is to liquidate a position or fulfill an obligation by taking an equal and opposite position (this will be explained more fully in Chapter Eight).

In Singapore, as in most other forex markets, commercial banks, through the OTC network, dominate the foreign exchange market. Banks have dealing rooms which employ foreign exchange dealers who trade with a limited pre-defined delegated authority on behalf of the banks employing them.

Banks trade for their customers, whether individual or corporate, and also with other banks or their own bank's agents or branches in other countries.

Central banks intervene in the interbank forex markets from time to time to smooth out currency fluctuations or to maintain agreed upon target exchange rates. In recent years Japan's central bank has intervened in the forex markets to prop up the US dollar against the yen, so the price of Japanese exports to the US can be kept down.

Round-the-Clock Trading

The world's forex markets constitute a global 24-hour currency market. They are in constant contact with each other and interdependent. By the time one market has closed, trading has begun on forex markets in the next zone.

Japan's central bank has often intervened to prop up the US dollar.

Trading on closing (previous) markets will also set the trading tone for those in the next time zone, especially when orders from one market are passed on to a later one. A good day on the New York markets will often boost opening trading on the London and European markets. And the mood of these markets can in turn set the tone for the Tokyo and Singapore sessions.

The Need for Foreign Exchange

Without forex markets global trade and commerce would grind to a halt. Money is as much a critical medium of exchange between nations as it is within them. A society without money is reduced to primitive bartering to conduct its commerce. The same is true between nations.

International trade normally involves an exchange of currencies as well as goods. Within a country buyers purchase from sellers with a common currency. However, the foreign seller of any goods or items must be paid in his own country's currency.

How does this happen?

Suppose a Singapore car dealer wants to import some Honda cars from Japan. He must pay the Japanese seller in yen. To do this he buys yen with Singapore dollars on the Singapore spot market and has the newly-purchased yen sent to the Japanese supplier.

Furthermore, every time an importer from another country buys yen to acquire goods from Japan he creates a demand for yen. Similarly, when Japan, for example, buys wheat from the US a demand for US dollars is created. In other words when Country A imports goods or pays for services from Country B the demand for the latter's currency increases.

Thus a Singaporean importer who wants to buy M$1,000,000 to pay for palm oil from Malaysia at a time when the spot rate for Malaysian ringgits is S$0.57 would need to pay S$570,000 for this one million ringgits.

During the day a currency's spot as well as forward and futures rate can change constantly. For example, if there is a sudden demand for Singapore dollars in Malaysia, the spot price for Singapore dollars will immediately appreciate or strengthen against the ringgit. When this occurs you can buy more ringgits with the same number of Singapore dollars.

If, however, there is a surge in demand for Malaysian ringgits in Singapore then the Singapore dollar will depreciate against the ringgit: you will need more Singapore dollars to buy the same number of ringgits. We will now look at the factors responsible for fluctuations in currency rates.

What Determines Exchange Rates

The factors that determine prices can be of two basic types: fundamental and market-driven. Fundamental factors relate to such concerns as the production (or availability) and consumption (or use) of an asset. Market-driven factors result from efforts to profit from an asset's price changes; when it is bought and sold to be profited from, rather than used. Since the early 1970s such market factors — mainly speculative — have increasingly determined the price of one currency in terms of another.

But first let us look at the fundamental factors, which have always been regarded as the main determinants of exchange rates — the price of one currency in terms of another.

FUNDAMENTAL FACTORS

These factors are many and varied and interact in all sorts of complex ways which economists are still trying to work out — with equally complex mathematical equations.

To complicate matters further, some factors can lift a currency's exchange rate in one way and depress it in another, often at the same time, as the following will show.

Balance of Trade

The balance (relativities) between a country's imports and exports is probably the most direct determinant of the exchange rate for its currency in terms of other currencies.

When a country exports more than it imports foreign exchange reserves will rise. Its stock of other countries' currencies will exceed the amount that it needs to pay for its imports from those countries and so it will experience a surplus. This will push up the value of its currency against other currencies, especially of those where its exports exceed imports.

Conversely, if a country imports more its foreign reserves will decline, especially against currencies of the countries it imports more from than exports to.

This is the situation with the US and Japan. Japan has been exporting more to the US than the US has been exporting to Japan. Put another way, Japan has been importing less from the US than the US has been importing from Japan. As a result Japan has a US dollars surplus earned from its exports to the US (and its failure to spend them on imports from the US) while the US does not have enough yen from its exports to Japan to pay for its imports from Japan. America has a trade deficit with Japan as it does with Taiwan and South Korea.

For these reasons the US dollar has (till 1996) been depreciating against the yen, the Korean won and the Taiwan dollar.

Inflation

Countries experiencing high inflation ("too much money chasing too few goods") will be importing more goods to satisfy excess demand.

To access these imports countries have to acquire the currencies of the trading partners they wish to import from. This creates a greater demand for the currencies of the exporters' and pushes up their exchange rates vis-a-vis those of the importing countries. In other words the exchange rates for the importing countries currencies will have fallen relative to those whose goods they are importing.

A country whose inflation rate is higher than that of other countries will experience a faster increase in production costs. This will make its goods more expensive, reducing export demand for them resulting in lower exchange rates for its currency against those of other countries. Also, rising inflation causes the country to import more, further depreciating its exchange rate.

On the plus side, rising inflation can lead to higher interest rates, which will attract an inflow of capital, strengthening a country's currency.

Conversely, deflation will lower a country's demand for goods and services because there is less money around to buy them. This means fewer imports, less demand for other currencies and a resulting appreciation of the country's currency against the others.

Interest Rates

Money is lent at different rates of interest in different countries. In Singapore interest rates on bank loans are usually about 5 per cent whereas in Indonesia and other countries they can be 25 per cent or more.

A country with high interest rates will attract investment funds from countries where interest rates are lower. Such differences in interest rates are termed interest rates differentials.

But while higher interest rates may attract funds to a country, other factors may cause them to flow out again. The country's currency may depreciate, cancelling out the profit that foreign capital may be gaining from higher interest rates and the investment funds exit to more promising locales.

Directly related to the level of interest rates is inflation, where countries with low inflation will have low interest rates and so be likely to experience outflows of capital and a subsequent decline in foreign exchange reserves. However, if the forex markets think a country's currency will appreciate, then speculative capital inflows could increase, even though interest rates may be low. This is the case with countries such as Singapore with its low interest and inflation rates.

Despite Singapore's low interest rates, forex market sentiment (especially of the speculative variety) may think that the Singapore dollar will rise significantly to offset the low interest rates offered here, with the result that capital flows into the republic. In fact much foreign capital that now flows into Singapore does so because the Singapore dollar continues to appreciate against most of the world's leading currencies.

Thus while initially high inflation rates in a country will push up interest rates and attract capital inflows, if market sentiment is that the higher interest rates will be cancelled out by a depreciating exchange rate (because exports are over-priced etc due to inflation), then capital will flow out of the country again. Conversely, low inflation and low interest rates may initially discourage foreign capital, but capital can still flow into a country if traders think that appreciation of its currency will offset its low interest rates.

Growth Rates

A rapidly growing economy will require more imports which means it will have a greater demand for foreign currencies, thus driving down the value of its own currency. However, high growth rates not only mean an expanding economy, but also rising exports. Thus the greater export earnings associated with growth will help pay for the rising imports that growth also requires.

Conversely, stagnant economies require fewer imports, resulting in lower demand for foreign currency and therefore less downward pressure on their own currency. But then one reason why such economies are stagnant is that exports are falling. Thus they may also be experiencing a drop in export earnings, which in turn weakens their currencies.

Productivity Growth

Above-average productivity growth is the sign of an increasingly efficient and competitive economy with lower priced exports, rising export earnings and an appreciating currency. Declining productivity indicates falling competitiveness, fewer exports and leads to a weakening currency.

Capital Account Flows

Capital account flows, which reflect the movement of investment funds in and out of a country also significantly affect exchange rates.

Such capital flows are of four types:

◆ *Corporate Investment* — where business enterprises establish new factories or other operations overseas, or buy existing concerns abroad by company take-overs.

♦ *Portfolio Investment* — covers the purchase of shares and bonds abroad by investors, either corporate or private and in either a country's public or private sectors.

♦ *Loans* — usually made by governments or banks to governments or businesses in other countries.

♦ *Overseas Borrowings* — where money is borrowed aboard at cheaper rates and then invested back home at higher rates.

Government Economic Policies

Government policies for regulating an economy, especially inflows and outflows of capital funds, can also profoundly affect a country's exchange rates.

For example, a government may launch policies that will encourage foreign investment and so attract more capital from abroad. Foreign investors will have to purchase the country's currency to send their capital into this country, causing its currency to appreciate against others.

Things to watch for include a history of devaluation and the chances of its government doing the same again.

Buying currencies of countries which have repeatedly devalued is risky. The value of any currency you hold could be slashed overnight.

Political Climate

Related to devaluation and government policies will be the political stability of a country. For example, the revolving door nature of successive Italian governments since World War Two has been reflected in the constant instability and repeated devaluations of the lira. France's political post-war instability from 1945 till the 1960s had a similar negative impact on the French franc.

Moreover, a country's political stability and philosophy will dictate how well it attracts or repels foreign investment.

Singapore's stable political climate has done much to attract large amounts of long-term foreign investment to the country.

Savings and Consumption Rates

When savings rates rise people will consume less and this is likely to reduce demand for imports.

This conserves a country's foreign currency reserves and maintains the strength of its own currency against those of other countries. It also creates a pool of funds for on-trading at cheaper rates, because the cost of lending funds is determined by access to funds.

Conversely, high consumption usually means a high level of imports, which will increase chances of large trade deficits and weakening currencies.

Tourism

Tourists from Country A who visit Country B will need to change their currency for that of B's while there. This will increase the demand for B's currency, pushing up the exchange rate for Country B's currency against that of Country A.

MARKET FACTORS

The central reality of today's foreign exchange markets is that one trillion a day is being traded on them and most of it has little to do with trade or normal investment. As Roberts notes in "$1000 Billion A Day":

"...no more than one-fifth of foreign-exchange business is for trade and investment. The other four-fifths is made up of the dealings of banks and other financial operators between themselves. They are trying to use money to make money."

It is this huge volume of largely speculative activity which profoundly distorts, if not negates, the operation of fundamental factors on currency rates. For example, in the 1960s Britain's monthly balance of trade figures were seen as strongly affecting the pound, but now they only slightly influence it on forex markets.

Again in recent years the power of central banks to hold currencies at particular levels has fallen dramatically.

Central banks normally hold the governments foreign exchange reserves, consisting of foreign currencies, gold and the right to draw funds from the International Monetary Fund (IMF) when necessary. When, for example, the Bank of England is defending the pound it might sell some of the US dollars and Deutschemarks in its reserves to buy sterling in the foreign exchange market to keep up the value of the pound.

But such strategies did not work in September 1992 when the BoE was unable to hold the line against speculators' attacks on the pound. Because the bank could not stop the pound's value from falling, the UK was forced out of Europe's Exchange Rate

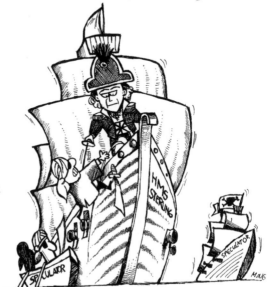

Britain has often had to fight off speculators' attacks on Sterling.

Mechanism (ERM). Ten month's later the combined forces of the Bundesbank (Germany's central bank) and the Bank of France — together with other ERM members — could not properly defend their currencies and keep them within ERM price bands. The result was that ERM was torn asunder and ceased to be an effective force for European monetary stability.

The world forex markets have become very volatile and subject to rumour, emotion and "gut feeling".

Market sentiment is often based on emotional perceptions of a currency. For example, if forex players believe a currency will fall and its government (and allies) do not have the will or means to support it against speculative attacks, that currency will probably fall. But a currency's exchange rates may hold if the market firstly believes that enough central banks from major countries have sufficient will and capacity to defend a currency.

Fancies for and against certain currencies can quickly develop. Once a movement starts rolling on a certain currency traders tell other traders and customers that they have: people start jumping on the bandwagon. In the process rational considerations of the fundamental factors that normally move currencies are brushed aside. As Roberts notes:

> "For a moment, the weight of funds behind a particular idea in the market, sometimes behind a fad, can drive an exchange rate far from what trade flows, relative competitiveness, price comparisons or interest rate differentials suggest it should be. In time, reality reasserts itself."

Though exchange rates may eventually reflect fundamental factors again, for months exchange rates may move strongly against such factors. The often adrenalin-driven behaviour of speculators makes them particularly susceptible to the emotions of fear, greed and hope, causing them to drive currencies higher or lower than more objective readings of the market would justify. A currency may be overvalued but, if enough people — for whatever illogical reason — keep buying, it will become more overvalued. At such times it is not what a currency's value ought to be but what the sum total of market decisions has made it that will be the critical factor.

The hair-trigger sensitivity of forex markets has been enhanced by the speed of communications which can accelerate the responses of market players. As a Swiss bank's currency economist said: "Technology has transformed parts of the forex market. With all those damn screens all over the world, people can act on things that they're very uninformed about, just like that!" Traders in New Zealand can be talking about the Italian political situation. Some news can hit the wires about the Italian premier and some people decide they want to sell lire. Such movements for or against a particular currency will quickly acquire a momentum of their own.

An awareness of the increasingly fickle and unstable nature of forex markets and how this can negate the effect of fundamental factors is critical for those who wish to trade on them.

Convertible and Non-Convertible Currencies

Normally the laws of supply and demand will determine the value of one currency in terms of another, but not always. In some countries the state will intervene to restrict, and usually distort, the process. At present there are over 120 members of the United Nations and most of them have currencies which can be freely traded for those of other countries. Such currencies are called convertible currencies.

However, some others, especially communist states (such as China, Vietnam and North Korea) do not allow their currencies to be freely exchanged for those from other states on the world forex markets and so have what is called non-convertible currencies. For example, while Myanmar kyats may be exchanged for US dollars, Myanmar government financial institutions and banks will not exchange kyats for US dollars. In other words they want to get as many US dollars as they can and to keep them to pay for imports sanctioned by the state rather than have their citizens get their hands on these dollars to spend on consumer goods for themselves.

Whether countries have convertible or non-convertible currencies will largely depend on the nature of their political systems and whether they want to exercise extensive control over the economy, or allow the free play of market forces to determine economic activity.

The same observations apply to countries which allow the value of their currency to be determined by a floating exchange rate (one determined by forces of supply and demand in the money markets) versus those who have fixed exchange rates (fixed by the government).

Myanmar seeks to impose a fixed exchange rate for the kyat against other countries so that the government can get the maximum amount of foreign exchange for its currency. Unfortunately, in such situations the currency may only be worth (in other currencies) a fraction of what the government thinks it should be worth. Inevitably the laws of supply and demand will assert themselves and a flourishing currency black market will develop where the local money will be traded for foreign currencies at often a fraction of the official rate. In Myanmar, as elsewhere, the exchange rate for a state-controlled currency such as the kyat on the black market more closely reflects the true demand for kyat in terms of other countries' money.

Forex Trading in Singapore

In Singapore, the US dollar is the currency most frequently traded. Others are the Malaysian ringgit and the Canadian, Australian, New Zealand and Hongkong dollars, British pounds, Deutschemarks, Swiss and French francs and Japanese yen. They are traded either on spot, OTC or forward markets or the futures market.

◆ *OTC Markets*

In Singapore, as elsewhere, the interbank market is for forward contracts and spot forex.

◆ *SIMEX*

SIMEX too trades in spot forex in the form of Deferred Spot contracts, which were introduced in June 1993. They are the Deferred Spot Forex contracts for the US$/Yen and US$/Deutschemark. These are among the most popular forex financial instruments in world financial markets.

SIMEX currency options are for:

◆ Euroyen

◆ Eurodollar

Useful References

"$1000 Billion A Day" *by John Roberts*

"All About Futures" *by Thomas Mc Cafferty and Russell Wasendorff*

"Directory of Personal Investment 1996" *by Financial Planner*

"Financial Markets and Institutions in Singapore" *by Tan Chwee Huat*

"How to Invest in Commodities, Gold and Currencies" *by Doreen Soh*

"Trading Asia-Pacific Financial Futures Markets" *by Will Slayter and Edna Carew*

CHAPTER FIVE

Interest Rates and Stock Indexes

*F*inancial instruments is the ungainly term used to cover foreign exchange, interest rate and stock index futures. Together they have largely fuelled the growth in derivatives over the last two decades.

Since the early 1970s the periodic instability of world financial markets has largely been responsible for the growing popularity of financial instruments. Oil crises, inflation and the switch from fixed exchange rates to floating ones have created unstable currency and interest rates, making risk-management and business planning increasingly difficult. Not only foreign currency, but also interest rate and stock exchange index futures have developed to help the financial and business community deal with this problem.

This chapter looks at interest rates (which in the derivatives markets are usually linked with foreign currencies) and stock index futures.

INTEREST RATES

Basically interest rates are the cost of borrowing money. Just as you pay for any other product or service, whether it be food, petrol or cars, you must pay for the use of money. This price is deemed its interest rate.

In the past, interest was always a "fee" for borrowing specified sums of money. It was merely the rate people were prepared to pay to borrow a certain sum of money. The rate charged was not an investment asset in itself. The asset was the interest-earning loan made by the lender. But over the last 20 years, interest rates have become financial assets in themselves. This has been a result of their growing use as hedging mechanisms and speculative mediums with the rise of the financial derivatives markets.

The Importance of Interest Rates

Since the mid-1970s interest rates have been traded as assets in their own right. Though nominally still linked to specified amounts of loan funds, interest rates they are now independent financial entities.

But how can an interest rate that merely registers the cost of borrowing money become an investment asset in itself like a loan? It becomes such an asset when it is used as the basis for hedging agreements. Under such agreements (or contracts) money must be paid from one party to another depending on whether interest rates rise or fall (this will be explained more fully below). In other words interest rates now no longer merely record the cost of borrowing money but form the basis of interest-rate hedging agreements. And these agreements not only stipulate when, and under what conditions money is to change hands, but can also be traded like any other asset. Furthermore, they become an investment asset, of the speculative type when they are traded for short-term capital gain.

Interest rates are now seen as central to most business and financial strategies. This is not hard to understand considering that interest rates represent the cost of borrowing money, a fundamentally important activity throughout today's debt-based world economic system. Interest rates are therefore a critical factor in most business and economic decision-making at government and non-government levels.

Because of their key importance, interest rates are a major barometer of economic health and have increasingly been used as a derivatives hedging mechanism by the money markets since the mid-70s. They reflect major movements in the national and world economy and so, through such interest rate derivatives as futures and options, they can be used to balance out any abrupt movements in interest rates that are likely to disrupt business or finance market activities.

Moreover, interest rate derivatives are also based on major world currencies as well as interest rates, thus making them an even broader reflection of the health of the global economies. Interest rate derivatives are linked to such widely-used currencies as the US dollar, the Deutschemark, the pound or the yen.

Interest Rate Derivatives

As with most derivatives, those for interest rates are of two types – futures and options. (There are other more complicated derivatives with new ones proliferating all the time, but they are beyond the scope of this book).

INTEREST RATES FUTURES

The world's first interest rate futures market was established by the Chicago Board of Trade in October 1975, and another by the Chicago Mercantile Exchange the following January. The main futures contracts traded on these markets were based on 90-day and one-year Treasury bills (T-bills), Treasury bonds, four-year Treasury notes and 30-day and 90-day commercial paper. Parties to interest rate contracts can in theory borrow or lend money at given rates of interest at a stipulated future date. By hedging with interest rate futures financial institutions, banks, corporations and business in general can stabilise their income and cash flow. A sharp rise in interest rates could severely harm a company's cash flow, impairing its ability to raise capital and carry out business plans. To reduce this exposure to interest rate risk the wise company uses interest rate futures contracts.

Theoretically such contracts are agreements whereby Party A agrees to provide loan funds to Party B at a specified interest rate by some future date. The buyers of an interest futures contract are obliged to accept delivery of loan funds and pay a specified rate of interest on them and the sellers to deliver these funds at this interest rate.

Such contracts, like those for currencies, are usually only delivered about 3 per cent of the time. Almost always they are "closed out" before delivery. No asset is delivered and the difference between the contracted price and the settlement price issettled in cash between the parties to the contract. This procedure will be described further in Chapter Eight on futures.

But whether closed out or not interest futures are used as a hedging device by banks, financial institutions and investment professionals. Normally no funds need be delivered for an interest futures contract (or in fact any futures contract) to fulfill a hedging function. Agreements to pay or accept a certain specified interest rate on a given amount of currency should delivery ever take place is all that is required. At, or before, settlement time the party who the interest rate market has favoured is paid by the other party who the market has moved against.

To understand this more clearly we need to realise that what is being sought here is interest rate protection, not opportunities to borrow or lend money. Hedgers who buy interest rate futures usually have all the money they need and those who sell them have probably lent all the money they have to lend. They simply want to be sure that they have not borrowed money at a too high interest rate, or lent (or invested it) too cheaply.

For example, a financial controller who has borrowed $10 million at 6 per cent for a year, does not want to see interest rates for such loans drop to 4 per cent in two month's time, and perhaps stay there for the duration of the loan. His boss will want his head. Conversely, a fund manager who has invested $10 million at 5 per cent for one year does not want to see the interest rate for that investment soar to 8 per cent a couple of months later. His clients will want his head.

Interest rate futures are a way of avoiding such unpleasant outcomes. For example, the financier can sell an interest rate futures contract on March 1, which will permit him to lend $10 million at 6 per cent up to June 1. The fact that he may not have that money to lend is irrelevant as far as the futures market is concerned. When June 1 approaches he can simply close out his position by buying a futures contract.

What does he gain? Well if interest rates drop to 4 per cent within those three months then the party he has sold the contract to still has to borrow $10 million from him at 6 per cent — which over a three-month period comes to an extra $50,000 ($150,000 - $100,000). When settlement time comes this $50,000 difference will be settled in cash with the buyer of the contract paying the financier $50,000. Thus even though interest rates have moved down the financier has $50,000 in hand to pay for the extra $50,000 he is now paying for the loan.

Conversely, the fund manager, who has invested $10 million at 5 per cent for one year, also wants to avoid being ambushed by rising interest rates. To avoid this he buys a futures contract which will in theory permit him to borrow $10 million at 5 per cent during the coming three months. If interest rates then rise to 7.5 per cent he can still theoretically borrow $10 million at 5 per cent. If he had not bought the contract he would have missed out on an extra 2.5 per cent interest on $10 million which over three months is $62,500. Again, when settlement time comes this $62,500 difference will be settled in cash with the seller of the contract paying the fund manager $62,500. On this occasion it has been the buyer of the contract who has been able to get the profit from the futures contract and put this against the interest missed when rates rose.

But this is only how interest rate futures work in theory. In practice though the fund manager would simply close out the contract by selling an interest rate futures contract. The mysteries of "close outs", and how losses and profits are settled will be more fully explained in Chapter Eight.

But another look at the above examples will further illustrate how interest rate futures work in practice.

First, what would have happened if the interest rate market had moved in the opposite direction for both parties? In each case they have lost money on the contracts they bought or sold. But if interest rates had gone up, the financial controller would have got a cheap loan. Conversely, if they had fallen the fund manager would have received a greater return on his investment. But in each case the use of contracts would have cancelled out such gains, in the same way as they cancelled out the losses when the interest rates moved in the opposite direction for each party.

Even so this would not worry each party, if they were purely concerned with hedging — that is protecting their position. Remember the first aim of hedgers is to obtain stable interest rates, not to try and profit from fluctuations in rates as speculators do. If this means they miss out on profits, the upside is that they also avoid losses. For them the goal is to have predictable, secure interest rates to effectively plan and implement business and investment strategies. Hedgers are risk-averse, not risk-takers.

With speculators of course the aim is to profit from price fluctuations in interest rate futures contracts, as with all futures contracts. Their presence is necessary in futures because they give depth to such markets. Without the speculators, turnover would only be a fraction of what it is, and hedgers would find it difficult to enter and exit the market easily.

OPTIONS

Options give you the right, but not the obligation to buy or sell an asset at the current market price some date in the future, including interest rate futures contracts. If the market moves in your favour you can exercise the option and buy the contract at the specified price, called the "strike price".

SIMEX offers options on Eurodollar, Euroyen and Euromark futures. Through the SIMEX options contract you get the right to buy or sell an options contract at a specified strike price.

This discussion of interest rate derivatives has sought to simply describe their basic principles. In the real world such derivatives come in more complex forms and combinations than outlined above. Nonetheless, it should be apparent that interest rates are not merely the cost of borrowing money. They are now traded as independent assets, separate from whatever loan funds or securities they theoretically represent.

Once this is appreciated the factors that move interest rates can be better understood.

What Drives Interest Rates

The number of factors that affect interest rates in an economy are probably about as many as those that move all other aspects of the economy. But, when assessing such factors traders need first to track the economy and pinpoint where they are in the economic cycle. Then they can more easily predict centralbank moves to keep the economy on an even keel.

THE ECONOMIC CYCLE

As we discussed in Chapter Two interest rates are usually dictated by inflation as well as overall economic activity. When the economy expands the demand — and therefore the price — for money increases. During recessions, the supply of money exceeds demand, causing interest rates to fall.

Interest rate traders must first track the economy.

You must allow for a "lag" affect with interest rates. Once a period of expansion is well underway the demand for money, propelled by its own momentum, continues after the expansion phase has subsided. Conversely, during the late stages of a recession, the supply of money exceeds demand, causing interest rates to fall.

Because changes in interest rates follow this cycle investors need to work out where they are in the cycle. As was indicated in Chapter Two commodity price movements are a good early warning system for rises or falls in inflation. But other factors should also be monitored to track the economic cycle.

◆ Overall growth and growth in specific sectors
◆ Inflation
◆ Spending levels

- Unemployment

◆ *Overall and Sector Growth*

The GNP has always been used to register the overall growth of an economy. Economic expansion lifts the demand for capital and pushes up interest rates.

However, growth in specific sectors, such as industrial prodution and construction, will have especially direct effects on interest rates. A rise in housing starts will often coincide with an increase in mortgage interest rates. Meanwhile, higher industrial production will lead to expansion of production capacities, greater demand for capital and will again lift interest rates.

◆ *Inflation*

Though commodities prices are probably the best early warning system for inflation, as Chapter Two noted, the most popular measure of inflation is the Consumer Price Index (CPI), which monitors the prices of finished goods. Rising CPI usually indicates an upward trend in the economy and likely upward pressures on interest rates.

◆ *Spending Levels*

A buoyant economy normally coincides with higher retail spending, which usually increases as an economy moves out of recession.

◆ *Unemployment*

Rising unemployment means a slowing economy and there-fore lower interest rates, yet falls in the numbers of jobless suggest an economic upswing and rising interest rates.

GOVERNMENT MONETARY POLICIES

Governments can strongly affect interest rates, through their central banks or similar regulatory bodies. In Singapore the MAS, is the central bank while in the US it is the Federal

Reserve. Central banks regulate interest rates in several ways:

♦ Increasing or decreasing the amount of money banks have to lend by varying the percentage of funds banks are required to hold in reserve.

♦ Varying the discount rate, the amount charged by the central bank to other banks when they borrow from it.

♦ The sale or purchase of government bonds and other securities on the open market. For example, if the Fed wants to drive down interest rates it buys government securities from dealers. This injects funds into the economy, increasing the supply of funds. If the Fed wants to push up interest rates it sells government securities, draining funds from the system, reducing the supply of money in the market place.

♦ In Singapore's case the loosening of restrictions on use of CPF funds has significantly boosted the amount of local money available for investment.

Thus tracking the economy and anticipating the likely government policies, through its central bank, are the first steps to predicting interest rates. But both tasks require skill that only comes with much practice.

SIMEX Contracts

Singapore's three interest-rate futures contracts, traded on SIMEX, are the Euroyen, Eurodollar and Euromark and are for three-month deposits for sums of US$1 million, DM1 million or Yen 100 million. The "Euro" prefix indicates the interest rates that European markets pay for these sums.

The SIMEX contracts, like most interest futures contracts, are not deliverable. However, on the Sydney Futures Exchange (SFE) and the New Zealand Futures and Options Exchange (NZFOE) such contracts are sometimes delivered.

The interest rate futures quoted in the Straits Times financial pages are 100 minus the interest rate. For example, a price of 96.04 means that the annual yield for the deposit is (100-96.04) or 3.96%. On this basis prices are inversely related to the interest yield. If interest rates fall the price of these futures contracts will rise and vice versa.

However, when buying interest rate futures in foreign currencies investors not only have to consider the interest rates of the country whose currency they are trading, but also the fluctuations of that country's currency. While the country's interest rates may be high, a fall in its exchange rate against the Singapore dollar, for example, would reduce or even eliminate profits from the interest rates.

MME Interest Rate Contract

So far the only contract offered by the MME is an interest rate contract based on funds lent between banks and other financial institutions on the Malaysian interbank market. The contract is a three-month KLIBOR (Kuala Lumpur Interbank Offered Rate) contract. The contract underlying asset is the three-month Ringgit interbank money market deposit. In other words, the contract's price will be determined by the fluctuations in the interest rate paid by this particular type of deposit.

The KLIBOR is an important benchmark used by Malaysian banks to price loans to the business sector and for pricing other money market instruments. The KLIBOR futures contract is the world's first Ringgit interest rate futures contract.

The contract enables banks, corporations and unit trust managers to protect themselves against Ringgit price fluctuations.

STOCK MARKET INDEXES (Indices)

Along with foreign exchange and interest rates, stock index derivatives have largely fueled the growth in derivatives during the past two decades.

Investors who want to trade on the movements of a stock market as a whole do so through stock exchange indexes, which are composed of groups of individual stocks on particular stock exchanges. This way investors have only to consider the factors that move the market as a whole — like inflation, interest rates and the other macro factors rather than those that move individual shares. Trading in shares of specific companies requires not only the consideration of these factors but also those that affect particular companies.

Stock index trading is done purely through derivatives (usually futures) contracts which are undeliverable. While up to 3 per cent of other futures contracts can be delivered no stock exchange index contracts are deliverable. Settlement is in cash.

Origins

Just as the world financial uncertainty in the 1970s and 1980s gave rise to interest rate and forex futures it also saw the birth of stock index futures.

Trading in stock index futures contracts began at several US exchanges in 1982. The first contract, introduced by the Kansas City Board of Trade (KCBT) in February 1982, was based on the Value Line Stock Index. The following month the Chicago Mercantile Exchange (CME) introduced the SLP 500 futures and then in May 1982 the New York Futures Exchange introduced the NYSE Composite Contract.

In May 1985 the CME obtained the right to use the Nikkei 225 and Nikkei-500 Stock Averages from the Nihon Keizai Shimbun (NKS). The agreement also included the right for these averages to be sub-licensed to SIMEX. As a result the Nikkei-225 futures contract was launched in Singapore in February 1986. The 225 is based on the stock prices of 225 companies on the Tokyo Stock Exchange. In 1987 SIMEX began trading the Nikkei-300 index which is based on the market capitalisation of 300 TSE companies. Since their introduction SIMEX's Nikkei-225 and 300 indexes have achieved considerable popularity with hedgers and speculators.

Again in 1993, SIMEX gave investors the opportunity to invest and hedge in the Hong Kong stock market with the launch of the

SIMEX MSCI Hong Kong Index Futures contract. The Hong Kong contract is based on the Morgan Stanley Capital International (MSCI) Hong Kong Index which has been tracking the Hong Kong market since 1970. This made SIMEX the only futures exchange in the world to offer hedging and trading opportunities in two of Asia's major stock markets — Japan and Hong Kong.

The KLOFFE contract tracks the KLSE's 100-stock Composite Index. The contract, which was introduced in December 1995, had a slow start. In the first year its trading volume only averaged about 500 contracts a day. At least 1000 contracts a day are needed for a futures exchange to break even.

However, at the time of writing Malaysia's Securities Commission was planning to allow stockbrokers to trade in derivatives, including the KLOFFE contract. Such a move was expected to greatly increase the contract's trading volume.

Who Uses Stock Exchange Indexes

As with interest rate futures the main users of stock index futures were initially portfolio managers in financial institutions. Stock index futures were a means of protecting the value of investments against stock market fluctuations. They offer investors a convenient instrument to quickly take long or short positions in the stock market as a whole. Stock index futures are bought and sold by a range of traders from individual investors and speculators to financial institutions, banks, corporations and superannuation and pension funds. Before share indexes arrived money managers could hold a well-diversified portfolio only by buying a diverse range of shares.

Compiling Indexes.

Overall market mood and sentiment are best reflected by changes in stock market indexes, which are a basket of shares and so express the general direction and trend of the market.

The construction of a stock exchange index is firstly determined by which shares are selected to make up the index. Here the aim is to ensure that a sufficiently representative sample group of shares are selected that accurately reflect the whole market.

Secondly indexes are shaped by how they are weighted. Should more importance should be given to shares that are widely traded? Or, companies which are important to the economy? Or, should each counter be treated equally and remain unweighted?

A base year is selected when devising an index and the price of the portfolio of shares selected is expressed as 100 points. A special formula is used to average daily changes to the portfolio and these changes are expressed as rises or falls against the 100 points base. Over the years, as a share market develops, these indices will often rise to several thousand points. For example, the base year for the Straits Times Index is 1964 (December 30) and at the time of writing it has reached about 2150. The Dow Jones in the US is 4700 and the Australian All Ordinaries is 2100.

The ST Index — the most commonly followed in Singapore — has a big influence on the market mood. The index consists of 30 Singapore and Malaysian blue chip industrial stocks. STI stocks are:

The ST Index is the most commonly followed in Singapore and significantly affects the market mood. Some 30 Singapore and Malaysian blue chip industrial stocks, free of weighting for market value make up the index. These are:

Construction and Building Materials Supplies
Lum Chang and NatSteel

Food and Beverage
Cerebos, F & N, Yeo Hiap Seng Manufacturing, Avimo, Gen Mag, IPC, SAe, SPC, STIC, Singatronics, UIC, Wearnes and Wing Tai

Printing & Publishing
SPH and Times Pub

Retailing
Metro

Shipbuilding/marine
Keppel, NOL and Sembawang Shipyard

Trading/Others
C & C, Haw Par, Inchcape, Intraco and Sime Singapore

Transportation
CWT, SBS and SIA

Telecommunications
Singapore Telecom

While the STI is the most followed index, there are many others used in Singapore. Another well-known one is the Business Times Composite Index of 40 stocks. The BTI includes stocks in all sectors, including finance and property. Companies are chosen because they are dominant in that sector and have enough public shares to make them easy to trade. Because of its wider base the BTI is a better indicator of the market's health.

In addition, the SES compiles the SES All-Singapore Index, based on all listed Singapore companies comprising the industrial and commercial, finance, hotel and property indexes. Because the All-Singapore index closely measures the price movements of all shares on the main board it best reflects the economy's overall state.

Other share indexes are compiled by banks and other financial institutions in Singapore. These include the United Overseas Bank Composite Index (a broad-based index of all stocks from all sectors) and the UOB Sesdaq Index; the Overseas-Chinese Banking Corporation Composite Index of 55 stocks; the Overseas Union Bank Composite Index of 50 stocks; the DBS 50 Index, and finally the DBS

CPF Index which gives the CPF investor a general idea how his stocks are performing.

In Malaysia, the most-used indexes are the KLSE Composite Index (CI) and the KLSE Emas Index (EI). The Composite Index was introduced in 1986, but with 1977 (starting from January 1977) as the base year. The CI represents 100 Malaysian blue chip stocks on the Main Board from all economic sectors.

The EMAS (Exchange Main Board All Share) Index was introduced in October 1991 and is based on all Main Board counters. The EMAS's base year is 1984 (starting from January 1984) and reflects broad market movements.

The KLSE also calculates indexes for the Second Board and also for:

♦ Consumer products
♦ Industrial products
♦ Construction
♦ Trading and services
♦ Finance

Other Malaysian share indexes are the NST (New Straits Times) Industrial Index.

Investors who want to track the market as a whole will use the more general indexes, while those interested in specific sectors can monitor the indexes specially compiled for such sectors.

Finally, there is the already mentioned MSCI, which was devised to accurately compare the performance of stock markets around the world against a common index. The MSCI has covered the world's developed markets since 1969 and emerging markets since 1988. It reflects 80 per cent of the world's equity capitalisation, covering 2700 securities in 22 developed markets and 1500 securities in 24 emerging markets. In Singapore, 38 of the SES counters are tracked by the MSCI.

Useful References

"All About Futures" *by Thomas McCafferty and Russell Wasendorff*
"Financial Markets and Institutions in Singapore" *by Tan Chwee Huat*
"How to Invest in Commodities, Gold and Currencies" *by Doreen Soh*

CHAPTER SIX

Commodities

C ommodities are processed or semi-processed raw materials used in virtually all the manufacturing and industrial processes of a modern economy. Traded commodities fall into three categories — agricultural products (usually called "softs"), metals and crude oil and its derivatives.

Softs such as coffee, cocoa, soybeans, pork bellies, rubber, palm oil, sugar and corn are traded on exchanges around the world, as are metals — either base (zinc, copper, aluminium and tin) or precious (gold, platinum, silver and palladium).

Over the centuries a global network of exchanges has developed to trade in commodities. However, as we mentioned earlier, the first modern commodities exchange was the CBOT established in 1848 to trade in farm products. Another was the CME (1919) for eggs and meat products. Together both exchanges now handle a wide range of commodities, as do many other commodities exchanges around the world, including those in this region.

In Singapore and Malaysia, commodities exchanges trade in palm oil, coffee, rubber and high-sulphur fuel oil and Brent crude. The Kuala Lumpur Commodity Exchange (KLCE) trades in palm oil; the Singapore Commodity Exchange (SICOM) also in rubber futures as well as coffee, while SIMEX trades in fuel oil and Brent crude futures.

As on the other investment markets, there are both spot and futures transactions. On the Singapore and Malaysian exchanges commodities are traded as futures contracts by hedgers or speculators. These contracts stipulate quantity, quality, price, delivery dates and credit terms for the commodities traded.

As on the other commodities markets the hedgers are usually producers, stockists and merchants or manufacturers who use raw materials. They primarily trade in commodities to lock in prices, so that they can be assured of buying or selling a given commodity at a specified price up to some future date. And as always the speculators trade in commodities to profit from price fluctuations.

We will now look at commodities traded in Singapore, Malaysia and on world commodity exchanges, describing each commodity's characteristics, production, consumption, price determinants and contract features.

Singapore Markets

Apart from gold (which will be discussed in the next chapter), the three commodities traded in Singapore are energy commodities (fuel oil and Brent crude), rubber and coffee futures. Energy commodities are traded on SIMEX and the rubber and coffee through SICOM.

OIL

Characteristics — In a refinery crude oil is heated till it vaporises. The vapour or gas is then distilled and cooled to a liquid form. This process separates raw crude into several petroleum products from lighter to heavier — butanes, gasolines, naphtha, condensates, kerosene, heating oil and residual oil.

Two key factors in assessing oil quality are density and sulphur content. Lower sulphur is preferred because it is less polluting. Lower density or light crude is better because it produces more valuable products, especially gasoline and jet fuel. Other important characteristics are: viscosity, pour point, colour, flash and heavy metals content.

Production — Major oil exporters are Saudi Arabia, Iran, Iraq, Kuwait, Libya, Nigeria and Algeria. Outside the oil cartel the Commonwealth of Independent States controls 5 to 8 per cent of the world's oil reserves and the US 3.4 per cent, but both the latter are also net importers. The biggest exporter of gas is Indonesia, which produces 40 per cent of the world total.

Consumption — Transport is the biggest user of oil, accounting for 45 per cent of consumption in Western Europe and 66 per cent in North America. Gas is often used as an alternative to oil, especially for power generation and cooking/heating purposes. Japan is the biggest market for liquefied natural gas (LNG) but long-term growth is expected to come from South Korea, Taiwan and Hongkong. Gas is mainly for power generation in the Asia-Pacific region, but in Europe it is mostly used for heating and its use fluctuates with the seasons.

Price Factors

◆ Conservation — High oil prices from the early 1970s prompted oil-importing countries, including the US, to implement energy conservation programmes which greatly cut fuel consumption and kept oil prices down.

But conservation programmes depend on how seriously consumers are reacting to pressure by governments and other bodies to conserve energy.

Threats of war and blockades will push prices up while peace and co-operation between nations will keep them down.

◆ Weather — In the northern hemisphere petrol is in greatest demand during the summer, while heating oil peaks during the winter.

◆ OPEC — When OPEC is united prices rise, but they fall when the members squabble. Till the Yom Kippur war between Israel and Egypt in 1973 oil prices were reasonably stable. But from then on the Organisation of Oil Exporting States (OPEC), which controls more than half the world's oil, has periodically been able to hold the world to ransom and dictate prices.

When OPEC states fight oil prices fall.

When OPEC states are united, oil prices rise.

OPEC however has often been divided with members refusing to stick to oil quotas while other oil-producing countries have stayed out of OPEC. This has often caused chaos in the market, creating both big opportunities and high risks for investors.

◆ Stocks — Plentiful oil stocks mean low prices, while shortages send prices soaring.

◆ New Discoveries —While new reserves will depress prices, high prices will re-open closed or inefficient wells.

Singapore, the world's top bunkering port, supplied 17.6 million tonnes of bunker oil in 1994 and offers several oil futures contracts through SIMEX. A couple of these contracts (the gas oil and Dubai crude futures contracts) have been discontinued, but at the time of writing SIMEX was offering the High Sulphur Fuel Oil Contract and in June 1995 introduced the Brent Crude Futures Contract under a mutual offset system with London's International Petroleum Exchange.

SIMEX oil contracts aim to meet regional hedging demands from refiners and oil traders. However, from early 1994 till the time of writing the fuel oil contract has languished because of poor liquidity and other factors. In mid-1995 SIMEX was considering revising the fuel oil contract's specifications to 3.5 per cent sulphur from 4 per cent to meet cargo trade specifications. Contract specifications for SIMEX oil contracts are:

SIMEX High Sulphur Fuel Oil Futures Contract
Contract Size –   100 tonnes
Quotation –   US$ per tonne
Min Fluctuation –   US$0.10 per tonne
Delivery –   9 consecutive months

SIMEX Brent Crude Futures Contract
Contract Size –   1000 barrels (42,000 US gallons)
Quotation –   US$ per barrel
Min Fluctuation –   1 US cent per barrel (equal to US$10 per unit)
Delivery –   12 consecutive months

RUBBER

Characteristics — Rubber comes from the sap (latex) of the rubber tree, which grows in Malaysia and other tropical countries. The latex collected from the tree is strained of impurities, coagulated into sheets which are then pressed between rollers to squeeze out as much water as possible and then smoked.

Production — At present Malaysia, Indonesia and Thailand are the world's major producers of rubber and in 1990 accounted for 73.4 per cent of global output. Synthetic rubber has been developed to compete with natural rubber since the 1900s, but is not of high enough quality to match natural rubber in the production of car, truck and aeroplane tyres. In 1992, 5.29 million tonnes of natural rubber and 9,160 tonnes of synthetic rubber were produced.

Consumption — The top consumers for rubber in 1990 were Japan (13% of output), China (11%) and India (7%). The tyre industry consumes the bulk of world rubber production.

Price Factors

◆ Because the biggest consumer of rubber is tyres the price for rubber will be greatly influenced by the growth and prospects for the automobile industry.

◆ The two biggest stock-pilers of natural rubber are the US Government, which has an estimated 127,000 tonnes, and the International Rubber Organisation, which does not reveal the size of its stockpile.

◆ Synthetic rubber is adequate for such products as batteries and electric insulators, but not vehicle tyres.

Contract Features — Traded by SICOM. The following SICOM rubber futures contracts are:

RSS 1 Contract

Contract size -	5 metric tonnes (single month), 15 metric tonnes (quarter).
Quotation -	Singapore cents per kilogram
Min Fluctuation -	0.25 Singapore cents per kilogram.
Delivery months -	Up to 18 months forward, starting with one month and followed by quarters.

RSS 3 Contract

Contract size -	5 tonnes (single month) 15 metric tonnes (quarter).

Quotation –	US cents per kilogram
Min Fluctuation –	US$0.25 cents per kilogram.
Delivery months –	Up to 18 months forward, starting with one month and followed by quarters.

TSR 20 Contract

Contract size –	20 tonnes (single month), 60 metric tonnes (quarter)
Quotation –	Singapore cents per kilogram
Min Fluctuation –	0.25 Singapore cents per kilogram.
Delivery months –	Up to 18 months forward, starting with one month and followed by quarters.

RCS Index Contract

This is based on cash settlements at maturity. No physical asset has to be delivered. The contract is based on a weighted price index from the Tokyo and Kobe rubber futures market.

Contract size –	One lot of 5000 times the RCS index
Quotation –	US cents per kilogram
Min Fluctuation –	0.1 cents per kilo
Delivery Months –	Spot month followed by eight consecutive months

COFFEE

Characteristics — There are two varieties of coffee — Arabica and Robusta. Arabica is of higher quality, with its better aroma and milder taste, and grows mostly in the cooler mountainous regions of South America. Robusta, grown in the hotter lower equatorial regions of Africa and Asia, is more disease-resistant and better able to withstand droughts and frosts.

Coffee trees bear fruit five years after planting. Harvesting occurs throughout the year. The coffee year runs from October 1 to September 30.

Production — Since the 1960s the world's annual exportable coffee production has ranged from 40 million to 90 million bags (a bag equals 60kg or 132 lbs).

World supply depends heavily on two countries — Brazil, followed by Colombia. Together they make up 50 per cent of world exports. Other major exporters are the Ivory Coast, El Salvador and Mexico.

However, the Robusta coffee futures contract traded by SICOM is for coffee traded from India, Indonesia, Vietnam and Laos.

Consumption — World demand is currently about 60 million bags annually. Major consumers are the industrial countries of the US, Canada, Western Europe and Australasia. However, US consumption is declining while that of Western Europe is rising. The demand for coffee is relatively price inelastic, that is demand is not strongly influenced by price. In many countries consumption has been stimulated in recent years by the availability of coffee vending machines and the promotion of instant coffee.

Price Factors

◆ Weather Conditions — These can affect the major producers, particularly Brazil. For example, a severe frost in 1994 and 1995 caused extensive damage to the Brazil coffee crop and pushed prices to record highs.

◆ Plant Disease and Pests — They can affect most coffee-growing regions. The most common disease is leaf rust. Generally however, Latin American coffee crops are free from damaging insects, unlike African crops which are often afflicted by many pests.

◆ The International Coffee Organisation's global export quota system is designed to maintain coffee prices within a defined range. But coffee market traders often trade against the ICO cartel, greatly minimising its influence.

◆ Coffee prices are said to move inversely to the strength of the currency in which they are denominated. For example, if the prices are in Sterling coffee prices will rise when Sterling weaken and vice-versa. The following Robusta coffee contract is traded by SICOM.

Contract Features
Contract Size – 10 metric tonnes

Quotation – US dollars per metric tonne

Min. Fluctuation – US$1 per metric tonn

Delivery Months – Any trading day of the delivery month

(On the London Commodities Exchange (LCE) the coffee contract lot is five tonnes and on the Coffee, Sugar and Cocoa Exchange in New York it is 37,000 lbs).

Kuala Lumpur
Previously the KLCE offered futures contracts for palm oil, cocoa, tin and rubber. But now the exchange only trades palm oil contracts.

PALM OIL
Characteristics — The palm tree fruit has a soft outer fibrous layer covering a kernel. The outer layer produces palm oil while the kernel yields palm kernel oil. Palm oil makes up 20 per cent of the fruit bunch and palm kernel oil about $2^1/2$ per cent.

Production — Malaysia dominates world palm oil production and in 1992 accounted for 54 per cent of global production ahead of Indonesia's 18 per cent and Nigeria's 10 per cent. Malaysia was responsible for 72.6 per cent of world exports in 1991 and Indonesia for 17.6 per cent. After being extracted from the soft outer layer of the palm fruit the oil is refined and leaves the factory as refined, bleached and odorised (RBD) palm oil. The oil is then subjected to a process called fractionation to split the liquid part called olein from the stearine and fatty acids. Olein is widely used as a liquid cooking oil while stearine is an ingredient in soap and preservatives.

Consumption — Major importers of palm oil in 1991 were: Germany (20.5 %), USA (16.9%), UK (9.1%) and Holland (8.1%). Palm oil has a 40 per cent share of the vegetable oils export market with oils produced from soybeans, corn, canola or rape seed and peanuts, composing the remainder.

Price Factors — As with soybean and coconut oils the prices for palm oil have dropped dramatically over the last 35 years. For example, palm oil was selling at $1800 a tonne in 1950 and by 1994 had dropped to $450 a tonne. Big advances in the productivity and efficiency of oilseed production and processing over the years have been the main reasons. However, to counter this trend palm oil producers have also managed to cut their costs to maintain the profitability of their operations.

Of all the edible oils, palm oil has been the most cost competitive since the 1980s. The surge of low-cost palm oil from South East Asia has cut into soybean markets. Currently, palm oil is the lowest cost vegetable oil on offer. However, effective campaigns against tropical oils by the American Soybean Association made the US public more aware of the need to reduce the intake of saturated fatty acids which palm and coconut oil are rich in.

As a result demand in the developed countries, such as the US, has been moving away from oils which are high in saturated fats, such as palm oil, and towards soybean oil and other oils low in such fats.

Contract Features — The KLCE trades the following palm oil futures contracts:

- Crude Palm Oil Futures Contract
- RBD Palm Olein Futures Contract
- Crude Palm Kernel Oil Futures Contract

- The Crude Palm Oil Futures for all palm oil refined in Malaysia, is quoted in Malaysian ringgit.

Contract Features –	25 tonnes
Quotation–	US dollars/Malaysian Ringgit per tonne
Min Fluctuation –	M$1 a tonne
Delivery –	The current month and the next five months, then alternate months up to 18 months ahead

- The RBD Palm Olein contract is an international contract quoted in US dollars.

Contract Size –	25 tonnes
Quotation –	US$ per tonne
Min Fluctuation –	US$0.50 per tonne
Delivery –	The current month and the next five months, then alternate months up to 18 months ahead.

- The Crude Palm Kernel Oil futures contract is a hedging instrument for the palm oil industry to ensure price stability.

Contract size –	15 tonnes
Quotation –	Malaysian Ringgit per tonne
Min Fluctuation –	M$1 per tonne
Delivery –	The current month and next 5 months then alternate months up to 12 months ahead

Other Commodity Markets

The following primary products are traded on commodities exchanges around the world. Singaporeans and Malaysians can trade on them through local commodities brokers who are linked to these markets.

TIN

Production — Tin is rarely used in its pure form, and is alloyed with other metals to exploit its poor conductivity, high resistance to corrosion and fatigue. These features make it an ideal protective covering for stronger metals such as steel, copper in the form of tinplate, foil and tubing.

Alloys containing tin serve many purposes. When mixed with lead it is used as solder. Tin is also found in ceramic enamels and organo-tin compounds such as plastics, wood preservatives, pesticides and paints.

Price Factors

♦ Because the use of tin is closely related to the demand for stronger metals, this demand will greatly affect the price of tin.

♦ Since 1921 an agreement by the Association of Tin Producing Countries (which includes Malaysia) has sought to stabilise tin prices by regulating output, exports and controlling stocks. But the resulting high tin prices have prompted consumers to use cheaper substitutes — copper, zinc and aluminium.

♦ At present tin prices are influenced by sales from the US Government tin stockpile and tin stock levels on the London Metals Exchange.

Contract size -	5 tonnes
Quotation -	US$ per tonne
Min Fluctuation -	US$5 per tonne
Delivery -	Daily to three months, then weekly to six months, then monthly to 15 months.

COCOA

Characteristics — Cocoa grows in equatorial regions at altitudes below about 350 metres and is used in the production of chocolate, confectionery and as a beverage.

After harvest, cocoa beans have to be processed and packed for shipment because they rapidly deteriorate in the tropical heat.

Cocoa trees can be harvested four years after planting. There are two crops in the cocoa year which run from October to September. The main crop is from October to March, the mid-crop from May to September.

Production — World production has grown steadily from one million tonnes in the 1960s to two million tonnes currently. Six countries, most of them in West Africa, account for more than three quarters of world output. The Ivory Coast is the largest producer, followed by Brazil, Ghana, Cameroon, Malaysia and Nigeria. Malaysia's production has rapidly increased over the last few years.

Consumption — The main buyers for cocoa are the more affluent countries of North America and Western Europe with the US being the largest importer, though total imports are declining. Other leading importers are Germany, the Netherlands, and the UK. New consumers of growing importance are Russia and Eastern Europe.

Seasonal Factors — Prices are lower during the harvest months of March and April. As cocoa does not store well in a humid climate, and because West African producers lack the capacity to process or store the beans, they export the crop soon after harvest. March and April are therefore the manufacturers' key buying months.

June and July prices tend to rise because that is when adverse weather and diseases are most likely to strike the mid-crop. It is also the time when manufacturers build up inventory for the Autumn production.

October and November prices however are likely to fall as commercial demand usually declines in these months.

Price Factors — Again the usual factors, such as production levels, whether actual or prospective, and shortages and surpluses of cocoa with the major producers will cause prices to fluctuate accordingly. Weather, especially drought in West Africa and the sub-Saharan areas in summer, cuts output and pushes up prices.

Cocoa can also be subject to a variety of fast-spreading diseases which also lift prices. Finally, cocoa is also said to move inversely to the strength of the currency in which it is denominated. In British Sterling, the cocoa price will rise when sterling weakens and vice versa.

Contract Features

Contract size –	10 tonnes
Quotation –	Pounds
Min Fluctuation –	One pound
Delivery months –	Mar, May, July, Sept, and Dec

WHEAT

Characteristics —Wheat is the world's oldest and most widely used food crop. It is of two types — winter wheat and spring wheat. Winter wheat is planted in the autumn (fall), goes dormant during the winter, resumes growth in the spring and is harvested in summer. Spring wheat is planted in the spring and harvested in autumn.

Production — The US is the world's largest wheat producer and each year exports more wheat than any other country. Other major producers include China, Canada, Australia, Russia, the Ukraine, Europe, Argentina and India. The US produces about one-sixth of the world's wheat. Of the wheat used in the US every year, between 25-35 per cent is milled into flour for domestic use in food products. A further 10-20 per cent is used for seed, fed directly to livestock or processed into various industrial products such as starch, adhesives and coatings. The rest is exported, usually as wheat, sometimes as flour.

Consumption — Japan has consistently been one of the US's biggest regular customers. By contrast the former Soviet republics have been noted for making big irregular purchases. Other large buyers include Egypt, South Korea, Brazil and Morocco.

Price Factors

♦ Initially wheat production, and therefore wheat prices, will be determined by two factors — acreage and yield.

♦ After the wheat has been planted and acreage established the market will focus on the weather to ascertain supply.

♦ Then the amount of wheat used for feed (which will largely depend on the prices of other stock feed such as corn and other feed grains).

♦ Exports will fluctuate depending on exchange rates and crop sizes in other countries.

Contract Features:

Contract size -	5000 bushels
Prices -	quoted in US dollars
Minimum fluctuation -	US$0.25 cents per bushel
Daily price limit -	US$0.20 per bushel
Contract months -	March, May, July, September and December
Last trading day (expiry) -	seventh market day before the end of the contract month

COTTON

Characteristics — Cotton is the fibrous overcoat of the cotton seed. The fibre varies in colour, length, weight and in several other ways. Types of cottons are distinguished by:

♦ Grade — based on three factors: colour, foreign matter and preparation.

♦ Staple length — upland cottons have medium and medium-long staples.

♦ Maturity (mike) quality — describes the maturity of the cotton and is measured by the airflow through the cotton. Cotton requires about 180 days of no-frost weather to grow. The crop grows best in hot weather with adequate, uniformly-spaced rainfall. Variations in these conditions causes substantial reductions in the size and quality of the crop.

Production — Major producers are the US, China, the former USSR, Turkey, Egypt and Australia. The planting season for cotton in the US begins as early as mid-March and as late as mid-June. Most is planted in April. Harvest time can be from late June to December. Most harvesting occurs in October and November. The crop year is considered to begin on August 1.

Consumption — Half the cotton used in the US is for the manufacture of cloth. The remainder is used for household and industrial purposes. Because of the consistent demand created by these uses demand for cotton is fairly stable.

Though the advent of synthetic materials has caused a drop in US demand, overall the worldwide requirements for cotton has remained largely unaffected. October–November and February–March are periods of heavy mill consumption.

Price Factors

♦ Seasonal — prices low during the Autumn harvest season, but subsequently high between May and July.

♦ Government Policies — The US Government particularly has had a strong support programme for cotton, though it is moving towards a more free-market approach and the industry will be receiving less government aid.

♦ The cotton futures contract does not lend itself well to inter-commodity spreads. The cotton spread is limited to intramarket spreads.

♦ Planting plans and acreage allotments give early indications of production levels and likely prices.

♦ Weather conditions during the planting, growing and harvesting seasons can affect the quality and quantity of the crop. For example, too little rain tends to retard germination and plant growth, whereas too much moisture reduces fruiting and causes late maturing.

Contract Features

Contract Size -	100 bales (50,000lbs) on the New York Cotton Exchange.
Daily limits -	US$0.02/lb Last trading day (expiry) — seventh market day of contract month.
Contract traded -	Cotton #2

PORK BELLIES

Characteristics — Pork bellies come from the side (or belly) of the hog. During processing the belly has the outer skin trimmed off and is cut into a rectangular shape. It can be frozen and stored for up to six months or processed immediately for consumption. The world centre for trading pork bellies is the Chicago Mercantile Exchange.

Production — The supply of pork bellies is determined by:

♦ Hog slaughter levels which follow a seasonal pattern, high in autumn and spring, and low in winter and summer.

♦ Belly stocks in cold-storage warehouses. Pork bellies are moved into storage in spring (largest movement) and autumn, but move out of storage in summer (usually continu-ing into October) and winter.

Consumption — Bellies are either sliced and sold as bacon or ground up and used as pork trimmings. While bacon is more commonly demanded the bellies are also minced and used as sausage materials when bellies' prices fall to the same level as pork trimmings. Bacon consumption follows a seasonal pattern, with higher levels in winter and during the BLT (bacon, lettuce and tomato season).

Price Factors

♦ The US Department of Agriculture's hog and pig reports on estimates for future pork production levels. The reports are quarterly, with the June and December surveys covering the entire US. The March and September reports cover only the 10 major hog-producing states.

♦ The levels of bellies stock in cold storage.

♦ The prices of grains, especially corn. Higher corn prices tend to push up hog prices.

♦ Hog slaughter levels which are used as a base to forecast bellies supply.

♦ The level of consumer spending. A depressed economy and widespread unemployment will mean less income and therefore reduced demand for pork and bacon etc.

Contract Features:

Contract sizes –	40,000 lbs.
Daily price limits –	US$0.02 lb.
Spot month expiry –	the fifth day before the end of the contract month, when the contracts expire.

SOYBEANS

Characteristics — Soybeans are primarily grown for processing into meal and oil. The meal is used as feed for poultry and livestock, while the oil goes into such food products as soybean sauce and curd, cooking oil and margarine.

In the Northern Hemisphere soybeans are harvested between early May and late June. Harvesting occurs from late September till late October. Optimum growing temperatures for soybeans are mid-70s Fahrenheit. August is a critical month. Good weather then can reverse unfavourable conditions, such as a drought in July or too much rain.

Every 60-lb bushel of soybeans, when crushed, yields 48lbs of soybean meal, 11 lbs of soybean oil and one pound of waste.

Production — Soybean cultivation began in China and Manchuria as a food crop. It then gradually spread to other countries. But during World War Two more countries began growing it as an important substitute source for protein food in Europe and North America.

Through the 1960s and 70s, as world demand for poultry, beef and pork soared, soybean rapidly became a favourite form of live-stock feed because of its high protein content. Also, growing consumer preferences for vegetable oils and margarine instead of butter and animal fats accelerated demand for soybean oil.

World soybean output grew from 61 million tonnes in 1976/7 to 100 million tonnes in 1986/7. The major producers are the US, Brazil, China, Argentina and Paraguay.

Consumption — Major importers of soybean are the EC and Japan; however, in Brazil's case the CIS is its biggest customer. While China is the world's third biggest producer of soybean, most of its production is used domestically.

For soybean meal, the biggest market is the US, which consumes more than 16 million tonnes annually, much of which it produces itself. The EC accounts for 50 per cent (11 million tonnes) of the world annual soybean meal imports.

Major consumers of soybean oil are the US (4.4 million tonnes), Brazil (1.6 million), and the EC (1.3 million). In recent years, though, the demand for soybean oil has declined because of competition from cheaper palm oil.

Price Factors

♦ US and Brazilian production. These are the two largest producers and consumers of soybean and soybean oil. Changes in the supply levels of either country have major repercussions on soybean prices.

♦ The US soybean supply factors are: planted acreage in spring; weather conditions in summer — the growing season; total crop production; levels of deliverable stocks in Chicago and Toledo.

♦ In Brazil, the growing season is January and February and should be closely monitored. Good crop patterns have a depressing effect on prices by early February.

◆ Mini-bull markets can occur when the acreage planted falls below "necessary" levels. Such markets occur 20 to 30 per cent of the time in midsummer, especially from droughts.

◆ Livestock prices have a direct influence on the demand for soybean meal and therefore soybean prices. When livestock prices are high, livestock operators will use more higher protein soybean meal instead of corn, which has more carbohydrates.

When livestock prices are high farmers will want their animals to be in the best possible condition for sale and so will feed them high-protein food to achieve this end.

◆ Demand for soybean oil depends on the price and availability of competing vegetable oil. For example, palm oil from Malaysia, can also be used in the production of margarine and edible oils.

◆ The US Government's corn and soybean programme. Corn and soybean are planted in the same regions of the US. Hence an increase in the corn acreage will reduce soybean acreage and vice-versa.

Normally a soybean-corn ratio of 2.1 to 1 or lower will reduce soybean acreage, while a 2.6 to 1 ratio will increase soybean acreage.

◆ Because a substantial proportion of soybean is exported foreign exchange rates will affect soybean prices. A strong US dollar will weaken prices because importers of US soybean have to pay more and so will be inclined to buy less. Conversely, a weak dollar will push up soybean prices because it will be cheaper to import soybeans from the US, increasing the amount of soybean purchased.

Contract Features:

Contract size per unit/lot at the CBOT is 5000 bushels (BU).

SUGAR

Characteristics — Sugar is produced from either sugar cane or sugar beet. Sugar cane grows in the warm, moist climates of tropical countries, while sugar beet grows in temperate zones. Sugar cane is harvested yearly with replanting necessary every two to six years. Unlike sugar cane, sugar beet grows underground. It is harvested every year and must be replanted annually. Sugar cane needs large and regular amounts of rainfall to grow. About 85 per cent of the cane's weight is juice, of which 11 per cent is sugar. Sugar beet roots grow below ground (over two metres) which enables them to draw upon subsoil moisture even in dry weather. However, very cloudy weather over an extended period will inhibit photosynthesis and retard the growth of sugar in the beet. The sugar year is from September 1 till August 31.

Production — Unlike such commodities as cocoa and coffee, sugar is produced around the world. Total production has grown from 54 million tonnes in 1963 to about 100 million tonnes since the early 1980s. Cane sugar accounts for 65 per cent.

Although sugar is a major world crop, most is consumed in countries where it is grown. The biggest exporters for cane sugar are Brazil, Cuba, Australia, the Philippines and Thailand. Beet sugar is mainly grown in the CIS, the US and Europe, especially France, Germany and Poland.

Although the yield from beet sugar is less, it is still big enough for fluctuations in EEC production to significantly affect sugar prices.

Consumption — Sugar is mainly used for food and beverage production, especially in baked goods, dairy products, soft drinks, confectionery and syrup products.

In the US food processing accounts for 75 per cent of sugar purchased while direct household purchases account for the rest.

During the past 20 years world consumption has grown consistently from 54 million tonnes to more than 90 million tonnes. The largest sugar consumers are the US, CIS, Japan, China, India and Mexico.

Previously, the demand for sugar did not change greatly with price rises. However, with the development of high-fructose corn syrup users have an alternative, making them more price sensitive. This factor can retard sugar price rises.

Price Factors

♦ Only 10 to 15 per cent of total world sugar is on the open market. Most sugar is produced and traded under preferential trade agreements between countries. Many countries, including those in the EC and the US, impose tariffs on sugar imports.

♦ Because the amount of "free" sugar on world markets is small, minor changes in total supply can significantly affect prices. Changes in supply as well as fluctuations of supplies can cause rapid price increases.

♦ The sugar beet crop in the EC countries fluctuates more regularly because it is harvested and replanted yearly.

♦ Sugar cane supply is relatively inelastic in the short run. It takes 18 months of growth before it can be harvested. Moreover, once planted, several cuttings of cane are likely even if the price falls — as long as production costs are covered.

♦ Weather and crop diseases can adversely affect sugar, like most other food crops. Hurricanes in the Philippines, rain before or during the harvest, late spring in temperate countries and drought or cold weather during summer months can all reduce output.

♦ The use and consumption of substitutes such as high-fructose corn syrup have also reduced sugar demand. Corn syrup has achieved almost total market dominance with certain types of soft drink.

♦ Oil prices can also have a slight effect on sugar prices because Brazil (a major sugar exporter) has encouraged its car owners to convert their vehicles to run on ethanol, an alcohol derived from sugar cane. When oil prices are high, a significant proportion of the annual crop is used to produce ethanol instead of sugar.

♦ An important factor in the sugar price is the level of sugar stocks compared with sugar consumption, expressed in percentage terms. A low stock-consumption ratio often leads to higher prices and vice versa. Historic bull markets of the 1970s were associated with ratios of 25 per cent or lower.

Contract Features — Contract size per unit/lot at the London Futures and Options Exchange is 50 tonnes and at the New York Coffee, Sugar and Cocoa Exchange is 112,000lbs.

❖ ❖ ❖ ❖ ❖ ❖

While many of the above commodities are not traded on Singapore or Malaysian exchanges, they can be bought and sold on exchanges in the US, UK and elsewhere through local commodities brokers. Here is a list of the main commodity exchanges and the commodities they deal in.

♦ Chicago Board of Trade (CBOT): Corn, oats, soyabeans, soyabean oil, soyabean meal, wheat and rice, as well as gold and silver.

♦ Chicago Mercantile Exchange (CME): Pork bellies, live cattle and pigs, and broiler chickens.

♦ London Metal Exchange (LME): Aluminium, lead, copper, nickel, tin and zinc.

♦ London Commodity Exchange (LCE): Robusta coffee, cocoa, sugar, wheat, barley and potatoes.

♦ New York Mercantile Exchange (NYMEX)

♦ Comex Division (merged with NYMEX in August 1994): Copper, gold and silver.

♦ NYMEX Division: Heating oil, gasoline, propane gas, crude oil, natural gas, platinum and palladium.

◆ International Petroleum Exchange (IPE): Gas oil, Brent crude and unleaded gasoline.

(The "Directory of Personal Investment 1996", published by Financial Planner, gives a comprehensive coverage of world commodities exchanges and the products they trade in).

In Singapore and Malaysia the notorious bucket shops often loom large in commodity trading. At the time of writing they can still trade in commodities. If you plan to trade in commodities make sure you are dealing with a firm that belongs to a commodities exchange, preferably one of the above.

Rubber and coffee (apart from energy futures traded on SIMEX) are the only commodities whose trading is regulated in Singapore by SICOM. At the time of writing no Singapore license is required to trade in silver, tin or palm oil.

This chapter has only given you the basic information about commodities. If you seriously intend to trade in any commodity you will need to know much more about it than has been described here. This chapter can only be a starting point.

Useful References

"All About Futures" *by Thomas McCafferty and Russell Wasendorf*
"How to Invest in Commodities, Gold and Currencies" *by Doreen Soh*
"Directory of Personal Investment 1996" *by Financial Planner*

CHAPTER SEVEN

Gold

"With gold anything is possible," says an ancient Chinese proverb. The metal's blend of rarity, durability and, portability has made it an ideal medium of exchange for most peoples and civilisations down the ages.

Currencies come and go, but those based on, or preferably made from, gold have always been the most prized medium of exchange. People everywhere have sought to possess gold as an insurance against war, revolution, famine and depression and other natural and man-made calamities.

Also, its extreme malleability makes it particularly suitable for jewellery. For such reasons gold has always attracted the feverish attention of the greedy and desperate.

In recent decades gold's special qualities have given it a wide range of industrial uses. Its capacity to resist corrosion makes it ideal for use in computers, polaroid cameras and transisters. Also, being one of the most ductile metals known (one ounce can be drawn out to over 1000 metres), gold can be used to produce thin, but strong electrical wiring.

Few other metals generate the same fever as gold.

However, gold's refuge for people's wealth in times of turmoil and uncertainty has given it special emotional price features, especially in modern times.

Gold's Special Features

Till recently the laws of supply and demand did not affect gold the way they do other commodities. The demand for money (inflation) was the fundamental factor that determined the price for gold. Investors around the world bought gold whenever they lost faith in money, especially such major currencies as the US dollar.

There was a clear and strong link between gold, international crises (political or economic) and the US dollar. During times of crisis people would seek refuge in either the dollar or gold. Normally, a crisis was bullish for the dollar or any other currency which was seen as a safe refuge.

When inflation eroded the value of major currencies gold looked increasingly attractive during times of crisis. Certainly, when inflation was weakening the dollar in 1972-4 and 1977-9, gold's price soared, rising to US$850 an ounce in 1980. But since the mid-1980s inflation in the US has been in the 1 to 3 per cent range and international crises have done little to markedly push up the gold price. In fact, from the early 1980s the gold market was bearish, having experienced a long term decline in the gold price from US$850 an ounce in late 1979 to US$329 a ounce in January 1986. In the mid-1990s it has fluctuated within a $380-$415 range.

However, it has not merely been low inflation rates since the mid-80s but the operation of new factors which have dimmed gold's allure. Gold appears to have shed its historical role as a metal that responds to world political and economic instability. Iraq's invasion of Kuwait in August 1990 seemed to prove this. The involvement of US and European forces in the conflict barely affected the gold price. As Doreen Soh, notes in "How to Invest in Commodities, Gold and Currencies":

"The reason for the absence of gold's historical quality of being a safe haven stems largely from the deregulation of world markets and the consequent growth of inflation-proof investment products. Gold in the 1990s is behaving more like a commodity. Its price responds to real fabrication demand for jewellery and electronics. Forward sellers, that is miners who enter into contracts to sell gold that they have yet to mine, determine the supply and place a cap on price rises."

If this view is accepted it would explain why gold has fluctuated within such a narrow range for the last decade or so. But gold still has some special supply and price features which could cause it to spin out of this price range in future.

Gold Price Factors

One critical gold price feature is the existing stockpile of gold. Allowing for the small amount of gold used for jewellery and other industrial uses, the current world inventory of gold is about 50 times its annual industrial requirements. If just two per cent of this came on to the market at one time the annual supply of gold would double.

Moreover, the annual production of gold is 40 to 50 million ounces — only 2 to $2^1/2$ per cent of the existing stockpile. And this newly-mined gold does little more than offset the gold consumed by industrial users. Thus, changes to production and consumption are insignificant compared with the huge existing stockpile of gold.

Consequently, new mining discoveries or uses of gold in industry and coinage affect the gold price far less than prices for other metals such as silver, copper and tin. Consequently, demand, rather than supply, is the major factor in determining gold prices. With supply being virtually fixed, the price of gold will rise and fall as demand rises and falls.

Till recently the main demand for gold was as a form of money, especially when the situation of the world's leading currency — the US dollar — deteriorated through inflation or during crises. Besides these two basic factors a complex web of other variables, both bullish and bearish, have significantly affected gold prices. They would do this by influencing inflation rates, or by directly affecting gold prices. The following lists of bullish and bearish gold price factors have been cited by such gold experts as Paul Sarnoff as determining gold prices. Doubtless many, perhaps most, would still operate, but to what extent under derivatives and other inflation-curbing financial instruments is hard to say.

Bullish Factors

♦ **Lower Interest Rates** — Gold in physical form ties up capital which could yield returns as dividends and interest to investors. However, when interest rates fall, interest-bearing investments become a less attractive investment than gold.

♦ **Disruption of South African Gold Production** — South Africa is the world's biggest producer of gold, followed by the CIS. If the production from these regions is disrupted because of strikes or political problems the gold price briefly rises till production is restored to normal.

♦ **Falling Soviet Gold Sales to the West** — Previously this was another bearish factor because the USSR was always a big holder of gold, being one of the world's biggest gold producers. From time to time the USSR would release bigquantities of the metal onto the market to pay for imports, such as wheat. But with the Soviet Union's collapse the CIS appears to have largely exhausted former Soviet gold reserves over the last couple of years to stave off financial disaster. Now the former Soviet republics have far less gold to release onto world markets, eliminating one of the bearish factors.

♦ **Increased Industrial Consumption** — Any evidence of increased industrial demand for gold also pushes its price up.

♦ **The Chinese Factor** — This could be an increasingly important factor as China develops and a growing proportion of its people achieve affluence and buy more gold. This could especially be so when China experiences one of its periodic bouts of political and economic uncertainty.

The same bullish factor is also developing in Indonesia, Thailand, Malaysia, Singapore and South Korea, where demand for gold has been very buoyant since mid-1993.

♦ **Buying by Central Banks** — They do this to increase their gold reserves.

♦ **Investment Demand** — Gold market traders have seen investment demand as being responsible for about 25 per cent of demand. Investors buy gold in the forms of gold bars and coins. But investment demand has been a reflection of other factors already mentioned here such as interest rates, inflation, international political tensions, the stability of the economic environment, economic growth (creating a greater surplus income and more money for investment) and falling rates of return on alternative investments.

♦ **Shift from Paper Assets** — This too has been seen as a bullish gold price factor, but one which could again have been due to the above-mentioned factors.

♦ **Oil prices** — The OPEC states are large gold hoarders. Their gold releases depend on the oil price. If oil prices rise they will not feel any need to sell gold to pay debts, keeping gold prices up.

Bearish Factors

The factors that reduce gold prices are mostly mirror images of the bullish factors just described.

♦ **Deflation** — With low rates of inflation, people have shown greater faith in paper money and have felt less inclined to convert it into gold or other tangible assets. Gold prices have been low over the past decade because of low inflation rates in OECD states.

♦ **Increased Interest Rates** — This can make interest-paying investments far more attractive than gold, which does not pay interest.

♦ **Expansion of Production** — Especially when undertaken by the major producers such as South Africa and the CIS.

♦ **Increased sales by the CIS** — With CIS gold reserves now apparently depleted this bearish factor will be less important on future gold markets.

♦ **Decreased Industrial Consumption** — Again decline in de mand for any items requiring use of gold, can be slightly bearish for gold.

♦ **Appreciation of the US Dollar** — When the US dollar rises against other currencies, the gold price has tended to fall.

♦ **The China Factor** — Any big slump in consumer demand for gold in China, due perhaps to a major recession, could curb this otherwise bullish factor.

♦ **Selling by Central Banks** — Central banks may decide to release gold on to the market for various reasons. For example, a country may be having difficulty paying for its imports, or may need to buy arms during a war. In recent years the former Soviet Union and later the CIS have had to sell gold reserves to pay for essential imports. Central banks sales could continue to be a powerful bearish factor as well as bullish factor, considering that they hold the bulk of the world's gold reserves.

♦ **Falls in Oil Prices** — When this occurs OPEC states may sell gold to pay debts, forcing the gold price down.

♦ **Lower Investment Demand** — Also a major factor but again largely a reflection of others.

♦ **Shifts to Paper Assets from Gold** — Any decisions by major financial institutions to move from gold to paper assets will be prompted by deflationary conditions, rising interest rates or greater economic security and stability.

Investing in Gold

There are three ways to invest in gold — on the spot markets, through derivatives (gold futures or options) or in gold mining companies.

The Spot Markets

There are two spot gold markets in Singapore, the Loco London and the bullion or kilobar market.

Loco London

Gold traded on the Loco London is 995 fineness, usually in bars of 400 ounces and in multiples of 100 ounces. As on other spot markets transactions can be carried out on a margin basis. Buyers usually trade on a 10 per cent margin, but they have to pay interest on the other 90 per cent financed by the dealer.

Sellers can sell short by borrowing gold from a dealer to sell to the dealer, who will then debit the client's gold account and charge him a borrowing cost of about 1 per cent. However, the dealer will also credit the client's account with proceeds from the sale. The dealer will then pay interest to the client on this credit balance.

Both purchase and sale contracts can stay open indefinitely without ever being settled. This arrangement in effect creates an undated futures market for the client. He need not worry about maturing contracts or taking physical delivery of the gold, provided margins are maintained to cover an adverse price movement against his position.

Bullion

Singapore also has a bullion or physical gold market — also called the physical kilobar market. The gold traded is 999.99 fineness and is therefore purer than London gold. Singapore gold prices are based on those in London but with a mark-up for the transport, insurance cost and profit margin, plus a premium for higher quality.

Kilobars can be bought on full payment for immediate physical delivery. However, buyers can also lodge gold bars with the selling bank for a fee, usually 1/8 per cent per annum of the price.

Buyers can also purchase kilobar gold certificates from the following five authorised banks in Singapore — DBS, OCBC, OUB and the Bank of Nova Scotia. Such certificates are for a standard lot of three bars, each weighing one kilogram of 999.99 fineness, and are valid for 12 months.

Smaller bars are also available on Singapore's physical gold market. Called "coin bars" they are issued or sold by various banks and gold dealers, including the Singapore Mint, and range from one gram to 500 grams. They are usually priced at more than the actual gold content to cover inscription and manufacturing costs.

Besides coin bars, gold coins can be bought in Singapore from the Singapore Board of Commissioners. Gold coins from other countries are also available. They include South African Krugerands, British Sovereigns, the American Double Eagle, the Australian Nugget, and the Dragon and Snake from Hongkong.

In addition, gold jewellery such as pendants and chains can be bought from Singapore's numerous gold shops in Chinatown, Little India and Geylang.

Derivatives

Singapore's SIMEX offers gold futures contracts, based on a contract size of 100 troy ounces. The United Overseas Bank and the Overseas Union Bank offer gold options, also on 100-ounce contracts.

Gold Shares

Buying shares in a gold-mining companies is another way to invest in gold. The share prices of such companies react immediately to changes in the gold price.

Useful References

"Financial Markets and Institutions in Singapore" *by Tan Chwee Huat*
"How to Invest in Commodities, Gold and Currencies" *by Doreen Soh*
"Trading in Gold" *by Paul Sarnoff*

CHAPTER EIGHT

Futures

*F*utures were originally devised as a hedge against uncertainty. But now they are largely a speculative medium on world financial markets. Futures are used in all investment markets and the assets being traded can be commodities, gold, foreign exchange, interest rates or stock exchange indexes.

Futures markets were initially meant to provide price and interest rate protection for businesses and entrepreneurs vulnerable to unexpected price movements in investment assets. Essentially futures allow risk to be transferred.

For example: a goldsmith may think the gold price will rise. To avoid paying more for gold he takes out a gold futures contract enabling him to buy a given quantity of gold at today's market price three months hence. If gold prices rise in that time he can still buy the gold at the "old" price rather than the current higher market price.

Through futures contracts businesses and producers can ensure that they will be supplied with a given asset — a commodity, foreign exchange or even an interest rate at a given date and price.

History

Futures markets are said to have originated in ancient Greece. But the Japanese are reputed to have developed the first proper futures trading system with the establishment of the Dojima Rice Trading Board at Osaka around 1730 to cater for the city's thriving rice market. Even so, modern commodities futures exchanges really only began with the founding of the CBOT in 1848. In subsequent decades commodities' exchanges for cotton, sugar, coffee, cocoa and other primary products sprang up in the US.

Till the early 1970s, futures markets dealt mostly in agricultural commodities and precious metals, including gold and silver. But from then onwards, as global economic instability created increased monetary uncertainty, financial futures began to be traded. This was due to oil price hikes, rising inflation and volatile interest rates, plus the move from fixed exchange rates to floating currencies in 1971. More predictable prices were sought for currencies, interest rates and other financial instruments. As a result, futures contracts and other derivatives were developed to protect against adverse movements in interest rates and currency fluctuations.

The first financial futures contract was for currency. It was initiated by the International Monetary Market, a division of the Chicago Mercantile Exchange, in May 1972. Then in 1975 the CBOT began trading interest rate futures.

Finally, stock exchange index futures were launched by the Kansas City Board of Trade, followed by the CME in 1982. Since the 1970s financial futures have taken off around the world. Futures exchanges in such major centres as London, Tokyo and Singapore were established to concentrate mainly or solely on financial futures. Today trade in financial futures has overtaken that for commodities and other primary products. Futures contracts exist for trade in three types of assets — commodities, gold and financial instruments (currencies, bonds, stock exchange indexes and interest rates).

Who Trades Futures?

Futures traders come from all major sectors of the business and banking community. They include exporters and importers, manufacturers, banks and financial institutions and individual traders. But they are of two types — hedgers and speculators.

As already indicated, hedgers seek to hedge or reduce their risk and futures markets were originally developed for them. A hedger is anyone in the commercial community who wants to be assured of stable prices, interest rates and investment returns to plan effective corporate and financial strategies.

While hedgers do profit from trading in futures, they traditionally regard such gains as secondary to reducing risk. Big financial institutions often speculate as well as hedge with futures as the Barings debacle of February 1995 showed. Most, however, do not like to admit it.

Besides this "disguised" speculation by the big boys there is the more open type practised by profiteers seeking to benefit from price fluctuations. Today most futures trading is speculative. Most commodities futures contracts, for example, are traded between myriads of speculators who would not know the difference between a coffee bean and a soybean.

Futures Markets

The main elements that make up a futures market are the futures exchange (which includes the clearing house) and the players.

The Futures Exchange

Most futures exchanges operate on the open outcry system, like stock exchanges did before the advent of computerised screen trading. They often have a lively trading floor and a public gallery. But the worldwide move towards electronic trading is likely to eventually cut out trading floor activity. Two futures exchanges which have operated electronically since they began are the New Zealand Futures and Options Exchange and INTEX (International Futures Exchange Ltd) in Bermuda.

All trading revolves around the futures contract — a legal agreement which binds both parties. The exchange sets the specifications of futures contracts and provides and regulates the trading venue — usually a trading floor. The exchange neither trades itself, nor sets prices for futures contracts.

Brokers (who represent exchange members), and authorised

independent operators (locals) gather in the pit to trade contracts. Under the open outcry method traders shout to each other and use hand signals to say whether they want to buy or sell and the quantities involved. A trade occurs when a bid and offer are accepted by each party.

The Clearing House

The clearing house, which works closely with the exchange, is the guarantor of performance for all contracts made on the floor of the exchange. It clears the trades, and matches individual trades and keeps track of the balances of members' accounts.

The Players

There are several types of operatives on Singapore and Malaysian futures exchanges. The general term broker would often apply to them.

Clearing Members

Companies which are members of both the exchange, through ownership of shares and seats, and of the clearing house.

Membership of the clearing house requires a large security deposit. They can act as brokers and clear trades directly through the clearing house.

Non-clearing Members

Companies who belong to the exchange, but not the clearing house. They too can be brokers and accept orders from customers, but they must have these trades cleared through a clearing member.

Associate Members

Companies who are also members of the exchange, through ownership of shares or seats on the exchange. They can trade for their own company's account or its subsidiaries, but not for anyone else. They too must clear their trades through a clearing member.

Individual Members

These are individuals who own shares or seats on the exchange. They are often called "locals" and usually professional speculators who trade on their own account. They must clear their trades through a clearing member and can not accept orders from ordinary customers.

Floor Traders

Those employed by clearing, non-clearing and associate members to carry out their trading orders on the exchange floor.

The Customer

Anyone, either a company or individual, who trades in the exchange's contracts.

Scalpers (or jobbers) trade on price movements as small as one tick and the narrowest of profit margins. They buy and sell positions within hours, sometimes minutes, for quick profits and are speculators pure and simple.

Scalpers act on the narrowest of profit margins.

Position players take either long or short positions depending on whether they think the market will rise or fall. They are concerned with following market trends rather than minor price fluctuations. They can either be speculators or hedgers.

Futures Contracts

Traditionally, futures contracts dealt in assets that are deliverable, whether they be commodities or currencies. Such contracts specified the amount and type of asset to be delivered, the delivery date or dates and place of delivery and certain options the contract seller has regarding the delivery process. For example, futures contacts specify a standard or fixed amount of the underlying asset. With currency futures, US dollars are always traded in lots of US$100,000 and British pounds in 62,500-pound lots, while wheat is traded in 5000 bushel lots and pork bellies in 40,000lb lots.

Delivery of the asset is usually on fixed dates in the March, June, September or December quarters. (Trading is usually carried out for delivery in these quarters and market activity is normally highest in the nearest month to delivery).

The Principles of Futures Trading

Whether speculating or not, those who acquire futures contracts are buying obligations to either receive or deliver the contract's asset — gold, pork bellies, British pounds or whatever.

Each futures contract has a buyer and a seller, a party who buys the contract and another who sells it. On buying a contract the purchaser agrees to take delivery of the contract's asset within a specified period (usually three months). The seller agrees to deliver the asset in that period.

As explained earlier those who buy contracts take long positions in the market. They are bullish because they believe the contract's underlying asset will rise. Conversely, the sellers, who are bearish take a short position because they think the asset's market price will fall.

Short traders
are bearish about
the market.

However, there is a lot more to futures trading than this. First you need to know how people make and lose money from trading. But to understand this you must first know how futures contracts work in theory, which the following examples will demonstrate.

In December, Tan thinks the price for gold (which is $385 at that time) will rise in the next few months. So, through his broker, he BUYS a gold futures contract from Lee, starting December 14. Under the contract's terms Tan must take delivery of gold at $385 any time up to March 14, from Lee. Even if gold goes up to $395 any time up to March 14, Lee must still deliver it to Tan at the agreed $385 price, because that is the price he already SOLD it to Tan for under the terms of the contract.

If, therefore, gold has risen to $395 and Lee thinks it will not fall before March 14, the final date he has to make delivery of the gold, Lee may think he should buy gold at $395, even though it is $10 more than he has received from Tan for the gold. He buys the gold (usually through purchase of another gold futures contract at $395) and delivers it to Tan, as required by the contract, and in the process Lee takes a $10 loss.

Tan on his part has received gold, now worth $395, but for which he paid $385 under his contract with Lee. He can now sell that gold at the current market price of $395, making a profit of $10. He would also do this through SELLING a gold futures contract for $395.

If, however, the gold price fell to $370 Tan, who has already bought it for $385, under his contract with Lee, would only get $370 for it. If Tan sells it, rather than wait for the gold price to rise again, he will make a loss of $15. But whatever the case he has lost $15 on this contract with Lee.

This is how futures trading traditionally worked when dealing with commodities, and still does on futures markets, especially those trading agricultural products and raw materials. But in the financial markets futures trading is a far more abstract and fleeting process. Perhaps for this reason so many people, including numerous professionals in the investment industry, find it hard to understand futures, or in fact derivatives in general. Leeson's comments during his interview with Sir David Frost in September 1995 support this view:

"...the senior people in London...didn't understand the basic administration of futures and options. And that was probably the biggest failing".

Later in the interview he said:

"A couple of people who were in the core places within Barings...had what I would describe as almost no understanding of the fundamentals of the business that they were supposed to be controlling. I mean futures and options is a relatively new business."

Similar sentiments were expressed by SIMEX chairman Elizabeth Sam, who said that while Leeson was "instrumental" in bringing down Barings, the primary fault lay with the bank's executives. "The main reason why Barings exploded was the failure of the Barings senior managers to understand the nature of the derivatives business," she told a meeting on the world's leading futures exchanges in Switzerland, a week after the Leeson interview.

Finally, here is a comment from investment guru, J. Mark Mobius. "Someone once said that derivatives are the work of the devil and even he doesn't understand them. The problem with derivatives is that there are just not enough people who really understand what derivatives specialists are trying to sell. On many occasions, regulators and money managers are taking what these people say on a lock, stock and barrel basis and it is a very dangerous game."

Damning words from those who know. But when one considers how abstract the futures trading process is there is little wonder that not only novice market players but high-level investment advisors have difficulty understanding its often slippery concepts.

Market veterans and professionals who do understand futures will probably find the following explanation over-long and unnecessary. But many such professionals who write on futures and derivatives do so in a manner that is often too brief and incomplete for beginners. The beginners tag could perhaps be applied to some senior Barings officials, whose failure to understand futures has cost them their jobs and reduced the once proud Barings to a subsidiary of a Dutch company.

To understand futures one's basic assumptions about buying and selling must be abandoned. It is an activity where paradoxes abound, such as the following:

◆ You sell something you do not have
◆ The asset you sell or buy (a futures contract) only comes into existence when you place an order to buy or sell one, and some-one else has placed a matching order to sell the same contract on the futures exchange.
◆ The asset mentioned in the contract is rarely, if ever delivered.
◆ You can enter the market by either buying or selling and you can leave the market by either buying or selling.
◆ You can trade with 10 to 20 times your capital because of the enormous leverage given by futures trading margins.

Let's examine each more closely.

Selling What you Do Not Have

One of the most perplexing aspects of futures trading relates to not only selling something which you do have, but which does not even exist — at least not till you have decided to sell it.

A futures trader who thinks the price of an asset will fall can sell a futures contract for it. If the price falls he can buy it at the lower price, after already having sold it at the higher price, and so make a profit.

For example, Tan decides the price of gold, now US$380, will drop. But how can he take advantage of this possibility? Well, with a futures contract he can sell the gold first at its current price of $380 and then buy it later at a lower price, if the price falls. If the price sinks to $370, and he has already received $380 he makes $10 on the transaction.

But how can Tan possibly sell something before he has bought it? Normally people buy something before they sell it — hopefully for a profit. Nonetheless, this form of reverse trading is not un known in the world of commerce. As was shown in the Introduction, A agrees to supply a car to B on a designated date and take a deposit on it from B. Then A can look for and buy a car for B. If, furthermore, B can buy the car for less than A has agreed to pay for it then B will make a profit from the transaction.

Transient Assets

A futures contract is always linked to some underlying asset, which can be anything from soya beans to interest rates. But the link is flimsy at best. At least 97 per cent of the time, neither party has any intention of delivering or taking delivery of the asset. And both parties will probably relinquish all such obligations within days, if not hours, of buying or selling the contract.

In theory futures contracts are agreements between two stipulated parties to deliver or accept delivery of a specified quantity of an asset. In practice, futures agreements are between a buyer or seller of the contract and the clearing house of the futures exchange. A brief description of futures trading procedures will illustrate how this is so.

Futures contracts are traded through floor traders who operate on the floor of a futures exchange. Offers to buy and sell are shouted out by brokers, complemented with hand signals, to indicate their intention and the quantities of the underlying asset required.

When a floor trader matches a buy or sell price with another floor trader, details of the matching trade are forwarded to the exchange's clearing house, which matches and registers the trade, which at this point becomes an enforceable futures contract with obligations — one party to deliver and another party to receive delivery of some specified asset at a given date.

Normally, these obligations would involve the buyers and the sellers of the contract, with one making and the other taking delivery of the asset, as the earlier examples showed. However, in modern futures trading this is not the case because of the role of the clearing house. Not only does the clearing house match and clear trades but it also assumes the obligation to deliver, or take delivery of the asset in a futures contract. In so doing it becomes the "seller's buyer" and the "buyer's seller", once the transaction has been completed.

Moreover, because it always matches up each buy and sell trade given to it by floor traders the clearing house will always have a buyer and seller for each contract. For every contract it must deliver there will be an equal and opposite contract requiring delivery.

The clearing house will never be stuck with unmatched contracts.

By breaking the link between buyer and seller and guaranteeing each trade the clearing house can ensure enormous volumes of futures contracts are traded daily. This gives a futures market depth and liquidity and ensures traders can enter and exit quickly and easily, an important consideration in any investment market.

Moreover, liquidity is enhanced because delivery of the underlying asset rarely takes place and not at all in the case of financial instruments on many futures exchanges including SIMEX.

In other words, virtually all futures contracts traded are merely matching market positions between buyers and sellers. They are not like normal contracts with designated parties with specified obligations to each other, where actual assets are delivered or taken delivery of. They are little more than bets or punts between a buyer and a seller on which way the market will go for some given asset. Moreover, differences are settled in cash, between winners and losers.

Entering and Leaving the Market

Another big difference between futures and other markets is the manner in which you enter or leave the market.

Normally, when you buy an asset, such as a share or other security, you have entered the market and are exposed to whatever price fluctuations your purchased asset is subject to. You leave the market when you sell and are no longer exposed.

Futures markets are different. You can enter the market by either buying or selling a contract by finding a matching trade and in this way you are exposed to whatever position you take. Similarly, you can leave the market by either buying or selling a contract, by what are called "close outs".

With close outs you take a position opposite to your existing one. If you have bought a contract you sell one and if you have sold a contract you buy one. In other words you have matched your own position. While you enter the market by matching someone else's position, you leave it by matching your own position.

When you enter the market by buying or selling a contract, you "open" a position. When you wish to leave the market you close that position by taking an opposite position. It's all so intangible isn't it? How do such fleeting transactions bear any resemblance to the futures contracts described earlier, where gold or some commodity was delivered or taken delivery of by one party from another? They both seem light years apart.

However, legally as far as the futures exchange is concerned, they are still essentially the same transaction. The only important consideration is that the transaction's contractual obligations are observed.

If a contract has been bought (someone has agreed to take delivery) then a contract must be sold (someone must agree to take delivery). Though the same person is performing both roles in the transaction this is of little consequence as long as the contractual obligations are observed. And the fact that nothing is being delivered is equally unimportant. You are dealings in obligations to receive delivery of an asset, not to actually buy or sell (acquire or relinquish ownership of) an asset.

You are merely taking a "position" in the market on some given asset. And you are buying or selling a contract for delivering or taking delivery of that asset, depending on whether you think its price will rise or fall. If you guess correctly you win; if not you lose.

Calculating Profit and Loss

But how do you collect your profits and pay your losses when trading futures? Initially such settlements are made through the clearing house. Being the guarantor for all contracts the clearing house ensures that profits or losses on each futures transaction are paid.

Once a trade has been registered by the clearing house, each party to the contract assumes their obligations with the clearing house, not with each other. Through the process of "novation" (a legal procedure by which one party can be substituted for another in a contract) a clearing house can match bought and sold contracts, enabling traders to open or close positions at any time.

However, the clearing house does not settle directly with clients, but with their brokers (if they are clearing members with the clearing house). If a broker is not a clearing member he has to settle with a broker who is. And then the client settles with his broker.

Thus the clearing house guarantees contracts to clearing members who in turn guarantee them to non-clearing members who in turn guarantee them to locals and clients. The latter must therefore look to their brokers for performance (See Chapter 15 choosing a broker).

Once a trade has been made, clearing members must pay a deposit to a clearing house the next trading day. If the price moves against the position originated by the clearing member then more cash (in the form of an additional margin) is required from the member to cover the paper loss. But when a price movement has favoured a position and produced a profit, payments are made by the clearing house to members. Then each settlement between the clearing house and clearing members is duplicated down the line between clearing and non-clearing members and between them and clients.

A computerised cash-management system ensures that debts between the clearing house and its members are settled daily. The clearing house always has a zero net position to enable it to settle profits and losses with each clearing buyer and seller as they liquidate their positions on behalf of non-clearing members and clients etc.

Clients' calculations of profit and loss can thus be made once they have closed out their positions or, on rare occasions, taken delivery of or delivered the underlying asset. Clients who have closed out a position and made a profit will have margins augmented by their broking firm, while those who have made losses will have them deducted from their margin accounts.

Settlement procedures for futures contracts can be better understood by examining how margins are used in futures trading.

Margins and Keeping Accounts

Margins are central to futures trading. They give traders enormous leverage (credit) to trade with. Most futures contracts can be bought with a 5 or 10 per cent deposit. This means a contract worth $100,000 can often be bought for as little as $5000, enormously magnifying any losses and gains. Margins will be discussed further in Chapter 15 ("The Mechanics of Trading").

Needless to say the availability of so much leverage lures many speculators into the market. This, combined with the standardisation of futures contracts features such as quality, quantity and delivery date of the underlying asset, has further enhanced contract turnover.

In summary, it could be said that a futures contact is little more than a matched trade between two parties when entering the market and each matching their previous trade when leaving it. Moreover, traders rarely hang on to contracts till they expire in three months time. Many traders, being speculators, may only keep them for a few days, often hours, before selling them.

Common Futures Concepts

Finally, no discussion of the principles of futures trading would be complete without a description of the following terms, which are regularly used in the industry.

- The basis
- Price convergence-divergence
- Arbitrage trading

The Basis

The basis is the current cash price for an asset minus its futures price. For example, a gold contract may have been bought for

US$375 on March 14 to mature on June 14.

Between those two dates both the spot gold price and the gold futures price will be constantly fluctuating. Sometimes the spot price may rise above the futures contract price, other times below it. If the gold price hits US$390 then the basis for this contract will be + US$15, if it falls to US$360, then it will be — US$15.

The chief determinant of the basis is how the market perceives the price prospects for the asset during the remainder of the current contract period. If the market is bullish about the asset during this period, then its futures price will be higher than its spot or current price. But if the market is bearish about the asset for the remaining contract period then its futures price will be lower than the spot price.

Price Divergence-Convergence

As a futures contract approaches its maturation date there will be less time and therefore less potential for rises or falls in price. As a result the futures and spot price will tend to converge as settlement day draws closer. In other words the basis will narrow.

When a contract has two or three months to run to maturity, there will often be a big gap between its price and the spot price. For example, a three-month gold contract due to mature on March 14 may have a futures market price of $385. However, the spot or current market price for gold (the underlying asset) may be $365. The futures price is $385 because the market expects gold to rise in the next three months.

However, over the next couple of months the spot price for gold may still be at $365 by early March. As the contract is due to mature by March 14, there is little time for the gold price to rise to $385. In anticipation of this the market would have been steadily marking down the price of the gold contract, so by early March it may only be $370 or less. Moreover, by settlement day, the spot and futures price would have converged to the same price.

Arbitrage and Arbitragers

Arbitragers try to exploit different rates, prices or conditions between markets or maturities. Arbitragers, seek inconsistencies between prices in different markets. When a stock or commodity sells for a lower price in one market compared with another, an arbitrager will buy it at the lower price and sell it at the higher on the other market.

Arbitragers often exploit the difference in an asset's cash market and futures price, just before a contract matures. Normally at such a time the futures and cash price have converged. But sometimes this is not the case. Anomalies occur.

For example, a security is $110 in the spot market, but the price of a futures contract for that security is still $111 at maturity. So the arbitrager sells the contract for $111 to the exchange and simultaneously buys the security in the spot market for $110. In so doing he has bought and delivered the security, purchased for $110, for $111 as required by the contract, making a $1 profit in the process.

Through simultaneous generation of buy and sell futures orders, pressures have been put on each market to cause the initial $1 gap between the futures and spot price for the security to narrow (or converge) to $0.

Arbitragers have been described as "price policemen" by ensuring that any price that is out of line is put back in line by the above procedure. Arbitragers do this by constantly searching for assets which are over or undervalued on respective investment markets. Then they pounce.

There is little risk to arbitrage trading, but because the return is so low, commission costs usually eat up any profit. Normally, only trading companies or floor traders who have their own seats on exchanges can successfully engage in arbitrage trading. Because they trade in such large volumes their transaction costs are low enough for them to profit from such trades.

Futures Trading in Singapore

Financial futures (forex, interest rates and stock indices), energy futures (fuel oil and crude oil) and rubber, coffee and gold futures are all traded on Singapore's futures markets. Except for rubber and coffee futures, which are traded by SICOM, the rest are handled by SIMEX.

SIMEX

The Gold Exchange of Singapore, which was established in November 1978 for the gold futures market, was SIMEX's predecessor. However, the reputation of the Gold Exchange was tarnished by lax supervision and an influx of shady operators. This situation worsened in the gold boom of the early 1980s when market activity and prices soared and investors were cheated, bringing about the exchange's downfall.

From 1982 onwards steps were taken to establish a more broadly-based futures exchange. The result was that SIMEX was set up in September 1984. It began trading with contracts based on Euro-dollars, currencies and gold. From its inception the exchange has been linked with the CME, through a mutual offset arrangement, which in 1984 was the first of its kind. Under this system traders could open in one market and close in the other. This not only gave traders extended trading hours, but increased risk management capacity, greater liquidity and reduced transaction costs. This mutual offset system, along with one established with the IPE for energy futures, has significantly boosted SIMEX's business. SIMEX now derives one third of its volume from the US.

SIMEX developed from a widespread belief that financial futures market in Asia would be an essential element in the development of regional money markets. With several countries in the Far East having such large foreign exchange reserves and the high activity of money and metals markets it was expected there would be ample business for a futures exchange in Singapore.

The global financial futures industry is growing rapidly and quickly extending into Asia in the 1990s. SIMEX sees itself as having a unique opportunity to spearhead the development of financial futures usage in the Asia-Pacific time zone. From its inception SIMEX set out to be an international exchange and never planned to rely solely on the Singapore market. By 1994 international participation accounted for 82 per cent of SIMEX's trading volume. Some milestones in SIMEX's development have been:

◆ 1986 (September) — Launch of the Nikkei 225 stock average contract and the addition of a Sterling contract. The launching of the Nikkei (a composite of 225 securities traded on the Tokyo Stock Exchange) was a world first for SIMEX. Never before had a futures exchange launched a stock indices contract on the Japanese stock market.

◆ 1989 — SIMEX was named "Exchange of the Year" by International Financing Review. It also won the same award in 1992 and 1993 — an unprecedented three times for a futures exchange.

Also, in 1989, SIMEX launched the Euroyen contract and the High Sulphur Fuel Oil contract. The latter has been a success because of the hedging demands of oil refiners and traders in the region.

◆ 1990 — Introduction of Euroyen options, crude oil futures and Euromark interest rate futures contracts.

◆ 1995 — Established another mutual offset system with the IPE, which represented the world's first offset system for energy futures.

SIMEX futures contracts available at present are for:
◆ 3-month Eurodollars
◆ 3-month Euromarks
◆ 3-month Euroyen

- MSCI Hong Kong Index
- Nikkei 225 Stock Index
- Nikkei 300 Stock Index
- 10-year Japanese Government bonds
- Gold
- High Sulphur Fuel Oil
- Brent Crude Oil

In addition, SIMEX trades deferred spot forex contracts in US$/Yen and US$/DM.

SICOM

Previously SICOM was the Rubber Association of Singapore Commodity Exchange (RASCE), formed in 1992. This was renamed the Singapore Commodity Exchange in February 1994 to better reflect its mission as a broad-based commodity exchange for the Asian region.

Instead of a trading pit the exchange's computerised trading system links market-makers and brokers. This gives them an efficient price discovery system, which ensures that all market participants get access to the best bid and offer. The exchange is promoted internationally by the Singapore Trade Development Board through its 26 offices world-wide.

At present SICOM trades four rubber futures and one coffee futures contract. The rubber contracts are the RSS 1, RSS 3, TSR 20 and the RCS Index contract, while the coffee contract is for Robusta coffee.

Futures Trading in Malaysia

To date, Malaysia's futures trading is still a small-scale operation compared to Singapore's. Malaysia currently has three futures exchanges, which each trade in one product.

Palm oil is traded on the KLCE, while its subsidiary the MME trades in interest rates and KLOFFE trades the KLSE's Composite

Index.

The KLCE

Since July 1980 the KLCE has been Malaysia's marketplace for commodities trading. In recent years turnover at the KLCE has increased dramatically and has reached 14 million tonnes of crude palm oil a year. Participants include producers, millers, refiners, traders and local investors as well as foreign firms and fund managers. The exchange's future looks bright considering that it offers the world's only palm oil contracts. When the KLCE's volume of contracts traded hit 600,000, a 160 per cent increase on the previous year, it became recognised as one of the fastest growing commodity futures in Asia. But as with most commodities exchanges only about 2 per cent of palm oil contracts are delivered.

Like SIMEX, the KLCE uses the open outcry trading method.

The MME

In August 1992, the MME, a wholly-owned subsidiary of the KLCE, began operations. MME trades KLIBOR interest-rate futures contracts.

KLOFFE

In December 1995, KLOFFE was launched and began trading a KLSE stock index futures contract. The four KLOFFE shareholders are Renong Bhd, Hong Leong Capital Bhd, New Straits Times Press (M) Bhd and Rashid Hussain Bhd.

A merger of all three Malaysian futures exchanges was mooted in May 1997 when the Securities Commission urged the exchanges to unite to save costs. On May 19, 1997 the chief executives of the KLCE, MME and KLOFFE signed a memorandum of under-standing to merge their clearing houses. At the time of writing no time frame had been given for the proposed merger.

❖ ❖ ❖ ❖ ❖ ❖

You can monitor SIMEX and SICOM futures prices through the Business Times and the financial pages of The Straits Times. At the time of writing, SIMEX were planning to release futures trading information on the Internet.

CHAPTER NINE

Options

As with futures, options originated centuries ago as both a speculative and hedging device.

Options made an early appearance during Holland's great tulip bulb craze, which reached its peak from 1634-7 when bulb prices soared to ridiculous levels due to speculative fever. In the last years of the craze people were bartering their personal belongings, such as land, jewels and furniture to buy bulbs, they hoped would make them instant millionaires.

To enhance speculative opportunities at that time options were devised which gave holders the right to buy tulip bulbs at their current market price during a specified period. Option holders had to pay a premium, which was about 15 to 20 per cent of the bulbs' current market price, for the right to take an option.

For example, if an option on a bulb worth 100 guilders was 20 guilders, then when the price had passed 120 guilders, the option would be worth exercising. Thus if the price reached 200 guilders, the option holder could exercise his right to buy at 100 and simultaneously sell at 200. He would then have made a profit of 80 guilders, after deducting the 20 guilders premium he paid. He had enjoyed a four-fold profit, whereas if he had bought them outright he would only have doubled his money. By use of such options people could play the market with a much smaller stake for prospects of a greater profit. As with the development of futures contracts, options, then and now, ensured far greater participation in the market.

Incidentally, after the tulip bulb prices rocketed to a 20-fold increase in January 1637 they plunged by an even greater amount the following month. Down and down the prices went till they were selling for little more than the price of a common onion, so ending one of the most bizarre speculative crazes in history.

However, options have continued to be a regular feature of investment markets and, with futures, are the main form that derivatives take. Futures trading involves obligations, while options represent rights (on the buyer's side) to buy and sell an asset at or up to a specified date. Like futures, options can be used for shares, financial instruments such as currencies, commodities or gold and also involve contracts.

Types of Options

Options are of two basic types — call and put options, which correspond to the long and short positions of futures traders. Call options for long positions are bought by those who think the asset price will rise. Buyers of put options take a short position, believing the asset's price will fall.

Besides buyers, there are also sellers of call and put options. They are called sellers of call and sellers of put and are also termed "option writers". Whether selling call or put options they have the obligation to fulfill the contract at the agreed terms when the buyer chooses to exercise it.

CALL OPTIONS

The tulip bulb example mentioned above was a call option, which gives one the right to BUY a particular asset at or up to a specified date and price, provided you pay a premium for the privilege. Buyers of call do not have to take delivery of an asset if they do not wish to, whereas in a futures contract they would deliver or else close out their position. By contrast the seller, or writer of the call option must deliver the asset if the buyer wants it.

Buyers of Call

Bullish traders are call buyers, believing the price of an asset, such as a share, will rise. For example, an investor may be bullish about International Unlimited. Its shares are currently $1 and a call option premium on them is 10c per share to have the right to buy them for $1 at any time within the next three months. This $1 price he can buy them at is the Strike Price.

If IU's price rose say to $1.50 during that time the investor could exercise his option and still buy them for $1. This will give him a 40c profit per share, after deducting the 10c premium. But if the share falls to 90c during the three-month option period he will not exercise his option at a cost of 10c per share.

But what if IU shares rise above the $1 strike price, but never reach $1.10, the break-even price? He would still find it profitable to exercise his option and buy the share. Say the share rises to $1.05, and he exercises the option and buys it for $1. If he does he makes 5c profit per share, but a net 5c loss after deducting the cost of 10c for the premium. But if he had not exercised his option he would have lost 10c per share.

Sellers of Call

The seller or writer of a call option must sell the underlying asset to the call buyer at the strike price should the buyer wish to exercise it at any time up to the expiration date.

The seller can make a profit if the market moves sideways or modestly declines. If the market falls by a greater amount than the premium paid by the buyer of the call option then he will not exercise the option.

If, for example, the premium on a $2 share is 10c and the share falls to $1.90 or even lower during the life of the option then the option will not be exercised and the seller will keep the premium. But that will be his maximum profit.

But he must deliver the share at the $2 strike price if the option's buyer wants it, which he would certainly do if, say, the share rose to $3. The seller would then have to buy the share at the current $3 price and deliver it to the buyer for $2, sustaining a big loss in the process.

PUT OPTIONS

Put options give you the right to SELL an asset up to a given date. For example, you may want to sell your house within a month, but want to be sure of getting the best price possible for it during that time. Mr Wong is prepared to pay you $500,000 for your house immediately. But there are other potential buyers around who might pay $550,000 or even $600,000 for it. But then again they may not. If you wait for them to make up their minds and then find they do not want your house, you may also lose Mr Wong who was prepared to pay $500,000 for it.

To solve this problem you can commit Mr Wong to buy with an agreement whereby you will pay him $10,000 if he agrees to buy your house for $500,000 at any time within the next 30 days, if you want him to. But you are not obliged to sell him the house during this period if you do not want to.

Mr Wong consoling himself with the proceeds of a failed options deal in his favourite karaoke bar.

You are still hoping that someone will come along and perhaps give you $600,000 for it and if he does you will be free to sell it to him. If the $600,000 buyer materialises and you sell the house to him then you will have forfeited the $10,000 premium you have paid to Mr Wong. But you have made an extra $100,000 by selling you house to the other buyer, which after deducting the premium, means your net profit from the transaction is therefore $90,000.

Mr Wong, though missing out on your house, has $10,000 in his pocket for the inconvenience and is free to look for another property. In the meantime, he can use the $10,000 to console himself down at the neighbourhood karaoke bar with a large bottle of VSOP brandy and his favourite hostess.

In such a situation you have bought a put option from Mr Wong giving you the right, but not the obligation, to sell the house to him at $500,000 at any time within 30 days. The same principles apply to put options in the investment markets.

Buyers of Put

Buyers of a put option have the right to SELL an asset at a given price up to a certain date, but must also pay a premium to do this. Put buyers being bearish, benefit if the market drops. By buying a put they have acquired the right to sell its asset at the current market price at some specified future date whatever its price at that time. If the asset's price falls they can buy it on the market at the lower price and then sell it at the option's exercise price which will be higher than the current price.

For example, if an investor is bearish about Global Enterprises shares he can buy a put option to have the right to sell them at their current price in future. If GE's price is $10, the premium is $1 for a three-month put option and if its price subsequently drops to $7 during that time, the put buyer can exercise his option, buy GE shares in the market at $7 and sell them for $10. After deducting the $1 premium his profit is $2 a share.

Sellers of Put

A put option seller has to buy the contract's underlying asset from the option's buyer, if the latter wishes it. And the seller will lose if the asset falls in price. As such, put option writers will sell a put option only if they think its asset will stay about the same or rise slightly. In other words, he must be mildly bullish about its prospects.

But like call sellers the profit will be confined to the premiums they receive from the put buyers. And again, should the price fall, they will still have to buy the asset at a higher strike price and sustain a loss when they sell it at the current lower price.

Though options are of two basic types — call and put — they are also classified in terms of whether they are American or European options. Both terms relate to the timing of the exercise of an option. Neither has anything to do with geographical location.

♦ European options permit the buyer to exercise his right only at a specified future date.

♦ An American option, however, allows the buyer to exercise his right at any time up to and including the expiry date.

American options are more popular because they allow buyers to exercise options at any time during the contract period.

The options we have discussed so far are of the American variety but there is nothing to stop two parties from entering into a European option. SIMEX trades American options.

Assessing an Option's Value

An option's value is its premium – determined by its intrinsic value and time value.

Intrinsic Value

The intrinsic value of an option is the amount it would be worth if it expired immediately. For example, if gold was selling at $385 and your call option gave you the right to buy at a $365 strike price, you would have an immediate profit of $20, which is its intrinsic value.

Thus for a call option its intrinsic value is the amount the current· market price of the asset is above its exercise or strike price. Conversely, the intrinsic value of a put option is how much its asset's market value is below the its strike price.

The terms: in-the-money, out-of-the-money and at-the-money are used when assessing whether or not an option has intrinsic value.

- ◆ In-the-money options are those which have intrinsic value. If they are call options their market or underlying price is greater than their strike price. If put options, the market price is less than the underlying price.

- ◆ With out-of-the-money call options the market price is less than their strike price and if put options, the strike price greater than the market price.

- ◆ For at-the-money options, both call and put, the strike and market price are the same.

Time Value

An option's time value is the difference between its premium and its intrinsic value. For example, the call option strike price for a share might be $5, its current market price is $7 and the option's premium on the share is $2.50c.

Thus its intrinsic price is $2 ($7 less $5) and its time value would be 50c ($2.50 less $2) per share. Again, if the put option strike price for this share was also $5, but its current market price had subsequently dropped to $4 and the option's premium on the share is $1.40, then its intrinsic value would be $1 ($5 less $4) and its time value would be 40c ($1.40 less $1) per share.

Time value reflects any additional amount buyers are willing to pay in the hope that changes in the underlying asset's price prior to expiration will increase the option's intrinsic value.

An option's time value is determined by:

♦ **The relationship between the strike price and the market price.** Deeply out-of-the-money or in-the-money options will have less time value money than options that are only slightly out-of-the-money, since it is unlikely that the market price will move to the strike price — or beyond — before expiration. Usually the maximum time value exists when the call or put option is at-the-money.

♦ **Time Remaining Until Expiration** — The more time that remains till expiration, the greater opportunity for price movement. This would be particularly important for an out-of-the-money option as there would be time for it to lift its price. At expiration options have no time value.

♦ **Volatility** — Time value will also vary with the estimated price volatility of the underlying asset for the remaining life-span of the option. More volatile underlying assets have higher option premiums than those that move within a narrower price range. The more volatile the price of an asset, the more potential for the asset to fluctuate widely in either direction. The increased volatility will enhance an option holder's chances of making large gains. For example, if you bought a call option and the market price quickly rises well above the strike price, you can exercise the call and reap a substantial profit.

However, if the price falls below the strike price and you do not exercise the option, your loss is confined to the premium you paid.

The same is true for put options, the only difference being of course that if the price of the asset falls substantially below the strike price then you will make big profits. Conversely, if the price rises above the strike price and you do not exercise the option then your loss is only the put option premium.

The above examples show that both call and put sellers make less profit, but they also expose themselves to far less risk than the call and put buyers. By contrast the latter stand to gain far more if the market moves in their favour.

It is a case of small risk, small gain for sellers of put and call options and big risk, big gain for buyers. The prospect of big profits for a small outlay is the main appeal of options' buyers. They can buy an asset at a fraction of its market price if and when its price rises. Their profit, which will increase as the asset's price moves in their favour, is unlimited. But should the market move against them, their loss is limited to the premium they paid for the option.

Options and Warrants

Both operate according to the same principles. As was shown in Chapter One warrants are written by a company for its shares. They are like call options which give buyers the right to buy the underlying security at an agreed price at any time up to the expiry date.

Usually warrants are given free to shareholders by the company to encourage them to buy more of its securities. Warrants give shareholders the right to buy the securities at a special discounted price, the subscription price, which would be the equivalent of an option's premium.

Once warrants are offered for sale on the open market, they can be bought and sold like any option at a premium price. Even so there are several differences between options and warrants.

- Life Span — While options have a life-span of no more than six months, warrants can be for three years or more.
- Call or put — Options can be either be put or call, but warrants can only be for call investors.
- Sellers/writers — Options can be written by anyone for a company's stocks or for any other security or other type of investment asset such as currencies, commodities or gold. Warrants, however, are issued only by a company to buy its securities.
- Company capital — Options for a company's shares will not increase its capital, but warrants will, once holders exercise them.

Options Trading in Singapore

In Singapore options for shares (stock options), interest rates, Japanese Government bonds, Nikkei stock indexes and gold are traded.

Share Options

These are traded through the SES. Introduced in 1978, they met with little success and were withdrawn before being re-launched in March 1993. The first two stock option contracts were Keppel Corporation Ltd and Singapore Airlines Ltd (Foreign). Subsequently options for City Developments Ltd and Natsteel Ltd were introduced.

The SES has set up a subsidiary, Option Clearing Company (Pte) Ltd (OCC), to act as a central clearing and settlement body for share options trading. All stock options traded are registered with the OCC, which acts as a central clearing and settlement body for options and guarantor of all trades.

Interest Rate Options

SIMEX handles two interest rate options in Singapore — the Eurodollar and Euroyen.

Bond options

Only Japanese 10-year Government bond options are traded in Singapore, again through SIMEX.

Nikkei Options

Options on the Nikkei 225 and Nikkei 300 stock indexes are traded by SIMEX.

Gold Options

Two banks in Singapore which offer or write options are the Overseas Union Bank and the United Overseas Bank.

Note

For a detailed explanation of stock options and options trading strategies refer to "Stock Options" (EPB) by Low Buen Sin and Lye Chiew Meng.

❖ ❖ ❖ ❖ ❖ ❖

Conclusion

The previous nine chapters outline the main investment markets. Investments offered on them range from the very safe to the highly speculative. Investors should familiarise themselves with all these markets and then decide which ones suit them in terms of outlay, time, risk and investment expertise required.

Once investors have chosen markets they want to trade in, they must then decide on a forecasting method or approach that will give them the best results. This is the focus of the next section.

Picking Winners

*P*redicting the future has been an abiding human obsession, especially when it comes to money-making. In the investment markets forecasts are the key to profit and weath. Prediction methods range from the superstitious to the scientific — and pseudo-scientific. It will not be possible to fully survey all the forecasting approaches used so we will look at the most widely used.

Two of the commonest approaches have been "technical" and "fundamental" analysis. Technical analysis appeared first, evolving out of the Dow theory that emerged about 100 years ago. Since then technical analysis has developed highly elaborate charting and statistical procedures for predicting future prices from past trends. Practitioners believe there is an innate and recurring pattern in the movement of prices which can be used to predict movements. But about 30 years ago growing academic research began to reveal serious flaws in technical analysis.

In the early 1960s, fundamental analysis came into vogue and still continues to dominate the thinking of many investment professionals. It seeks to discover and assess the vast range of economic and other factors that affect the prices of investments, to discover their "true" value. But by the 1970s the reputation of fundamental analysis had also been severely tarnished by academic research.

In its wake came the Efficient Market Hypothesis, but defects have been found in this theory too. Meanwhile, the "Contrarian" approach began to gain prominence. When aligned with psychological insights into market behaviour this approach shows some promise.

This section describes all the above approaches and concludes with a forecasting strategy which takes the best from each. But first technical analysis is outlined.

CHAPTER TEN

Technical Analysis

*T*he origins of technical analysis can be found in Dow Theory which was developed in the US at the turn of the century by Charles Dow. This theory emerged from the invention of the ticker tape machine which spewed out price and volume information on the share market. Many followers of the ticker tape believed they saw price patterns in the data and so began one of the first methods of technical analysis.

Since then more sophisticated methods of analysing price and volume data have been developed to predict prices. But studying price fluctuations is still the essence of the technical approach. And it is based on the belief that there are some innate pattern to these fluctuations which can be used to predict future price movements.

Nowadays technical analysts construct and use charts to depict price movements. They work on the assumption that past patterns will be repeated, enabling investors to profit. They believe previous information on prices and trading volume gives the enlightened trader a "picture" of the future.

The technical analyst claims that the price of a security or other asset depends on the supply and demand for it, which may have little relationship to its real value. Price is governed by basic economic, political and psychological inputs so numerous and complex that no individual can hope to understand and measure them all correctly.

The only useful information is that provided by price and volume statistics, from which technicians devise point and figure charts, moving averages and trendlines etc.

The Technicians' Three Premises

Technical analysis is based on the following:

◆ Market action discounts everything
◆ Prices move in trends
◆ History repeats itself.

Market Action Discounts Everything

Technicians believe anything that can possibly affect an asset's price — whether it be economic, political or psychological — is reflected in its price. Charts reflect the combined results of these forces on prices, including the market's mood.

Prices Move in Trends

A technician aims to plot price movements to identify market trends he can exploit till they weaken or reverse.

History Repeats Itself

The technical approach has been developed from the study of price movements over the last century. Technicians believe they have identified clear repeat patterns which reveal the bullish or bearish mood of the market. By use of these trends investors beleive they can predict market movements and will know when to buy or sell. The theory is that one can forecast future market behaviour by studying the past because the future is merely a reflection of the past.

Umm... Mr Lee... do you think this is the best way to deal with your bull market fetish.

FREUD AND JUNG PSYCHO-THERAPISTS

The Basics of Technical Analysis

Broadly speaking there are five aspects to technical analysis:

◆ Market trends

◆ Support and resistance levels

◆ Pattern recognition and the detection of support and resistance levels

◆ Volume and degree of open interest displayed

◆ Computerised trading methods

MARKET TRENDS

One of the first rules of technical analysis is that "the trend is your friend", or "always trade in the direction of the trend". The trend is the market's direction.

Markets do not move in a straight line, they move in three main directions — up, down or sideways.

Fig 1 depicts an upward trend with ascending peaks and troughs.

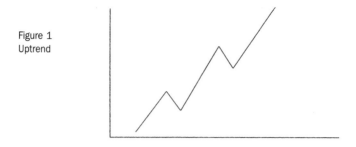

Figure 1
Uptrend

Fig. 2 below shows a downward trend with descending peaks and troughs.

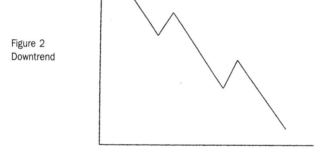

Figure 2
Downtrend

Meanwhile, Fig. 3 illustrates a sideways trend with horizontal peaks and troughs.

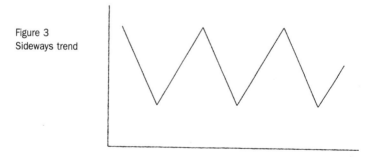

Figure 3
Sideways trend

An uptrend is a series of successively higher peaks and shallower troughs, while a downtrend is a series of declining peaks and deeper troughs. A pattern of horizontal peaks and troughs produce a sideways price trend, which represents a price equilibrium where supply and demand are more or less balanced. This is termed a flat market.

Obviously when the market trend is rising a buying strategy is best, when falling a selling strategy is preferable and when moving sideways, the do nothing strategy is appropriate.

Trends are broken down into three categories — the major, intermediate and the near-term. The major trend covers periods over six months, the intermediate three weeks to six months and the near-term anything less than three weeks.

In addition to these two market trends technicians look for retracements and channel lines.

Retracements

During the course of a general trend, prices will usually counter-trend on occasion — in other words they will move back against a portion of the current trend before resuming the original direction. These retracements are classified according to whether they represent a 33%, 50% or 66% counter-trend.

For example, if a price goes from $2 to $3 in a major move up, then starts to slide, the trader may think that this represents the beginning of a 50% retracement. He may then decide to sell out in anticipation that the price will drop to about $2.50 and then buy in again.

If the overall trend is to be maintained, however, the retracement must stop at the two-thirds point. If it does not then the trend may not merely be a tracement but one swinging into reverse.

Channel Lines

Sometimes prices trend within a clear cut range between the main trendline and another parallel line, called channel lines (Fig 4).

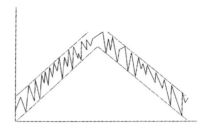

Figure 4
Channel lines

SUPPORT AND RESISTANCE LEVELS

Another main concern of technicians is to detect support and resistance levels (Fig. 5 below)

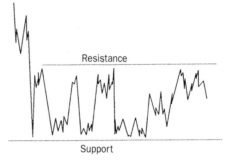

Figure 5
Support and resistance

Support occurs when there is a level or area on the market chart where buying pressure is strong enough to overcome selling pressure. As a result, a decline is halted and prices move up again. Usually a support level is identified by seeing where a previous downswing stopped before going up again.

Resistance occurs when selling pressure overcomes buying pressure and a price advance is turned back. Usually such a resistance point is identified from a previous price peak.

Technicians see the identification of both support and resistance levels as a potentially profitable piece of information. With it they try to sell just before the resistance point is reached. Similarly, technicians claim that it makes sense to try and buy just above a support level. Even traders will place "stop loss" orders just below the resistance (or support) level, so that if the price does unexpectedly break through, their loss will be minimised.

Support and resistance levels often reverse their roles once they have been significantly penetrated by price movements. When penetrated by upwards movements, resistance becomes support. (Fig. 6). Support, after being penetrated, becomes resistance. (Fig. 7).

Figure 6
Resistance become support

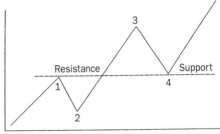

Figure 7
Support become resistance

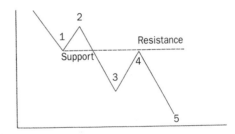

PATTERN RECOGNITION

Besides market trends and support and resistance levels, technicians contend there are several major patterns investors can use for forecasting. Such patterns, to be useful, have to be detected before the market moves the way they are indicating. If they are detected after the market has moved they merely confirm what has happened. But such patterns must occur sufficiently often to be of use in forecasting price movements.

Two basic patterns to watch for are continuation and reversal patterns.

Continuation Patterns

Patterns of this type will indicate whether a particular trend will continue. They are of two types:

Flag Patterns

These are used to identify a sharp movement, up or down, which represents the "pole". This is followed by a parallel or downwards movement, confined within two relatively narrow parallel lines, which completes a "flag" (Fig. 8). A technician will look to see whether the price will break out of its flag in the same direction as the preceding "pole". If this occurs he expects further movement to be of the same magnitude as the preceding "pole".

Figure 8
Flag and pole

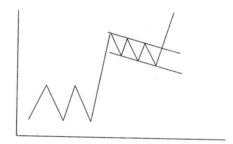

Triangles

These are of three types: ascending, descending and symmetrical. The ascending triangle has a flat upper boundary and a rising lower boundary (see Fig 9). This is a bullish pattern and indicates that buyers are more aggressive than sellers. The break-out usually occurs on the upside.

Figure 9
Ascending triangle

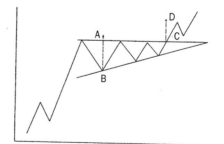

A descending triangle is just the opposite. It has a flat lower boundary and a descending upper boundary (see Fig 10). It indicates sellers are more aggressive than buyers and that the breakout will probably occur on the downside.

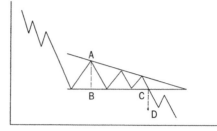

Figure 10
Decending triangle

A symmetrical triangle shows two converging trendlines, the upper line descending and the lower line ascending (See Fig 11). The vertical line at the left, measuring the pattern's height, is called the base. The point of intersection at the right, where the two lines meet, is called the apex. It represents a pause in the existing trend before the original trend resumes.

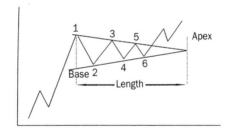

Figure 11
Symmetrical triangle

Reversal Patterns

These are of three types:

Head and Shoulders Reversal Pattern

Technicians see this as probably the best known and most reliable reversal pattern. Figure 12 depicts a graph showing a price rising for some time, at the left shoulder. Profit-taking has caused the price to drop. The price has then risen again steeply to the head before more profit-taking causes the price to drop more or less to the same level as before (the neck).

Although the price rises the gains are not as great as they were at the head.

The level of the right shoulder together with the frequent dips down to the next suggests to technicians that the previously observed upward trend is over and a fall is imminent. The breach of the neckline is the indication to sell.

The head and shoulders pattern are recognised periodically and technicians believe they are a useful predictive device. This pattern can also appear "upside-down" with inverse head and shoulders.

Figure 12
Head and shoulders

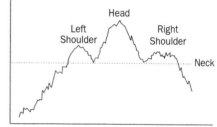

Double Tops and Bottoms

A double top is an indication of a trend reversal. A price could have been rising steadily for some time, then fallen as some investors sold to realise profits. It then has risen to its maximum level for a second time before starting to fall again. From such a double top the technician would predict that the trend has reversed. A typical double top is depicted below:

Figure 13
Double top (M)

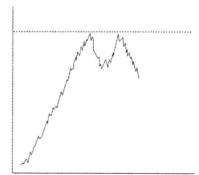

A double bottom is a mirror image of a double top (Fig 14).

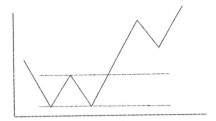

Figure 14
Double bottom (W)

Triple Tops and Bottoms

A triple top is similar to the head and shoulders configuration except that all peaks are at the same level. Each rally peak should be on lighter volume (Fig. 15). The pattern is complete when both troughs have been broken on heavier volume.

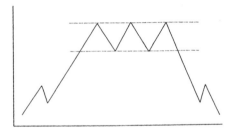

Figure 15
A triple top

A triple bottom is also similar to a head and shoulders and a mirror image of the triple top, with each low at the same level (Fig. 16).

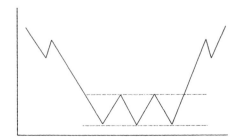

Figure 16
A triple bottom

VOLUME AND OPEN INTEREST

Both these indicators provide a good background to market activity. But while volume relates to all investment markets open interest is confined to futures and options. Volume describes market turnover generally, while open interest reflects the number of a market's futures or options contracts which have not yet been liquidated by an offsetting transaction or fulfilled by delivery.

Volume

The basic rules for volume analysis are:

♦ When prices are rising and volume increasing, the price will continue to rise and the uptrend is technically strong.

♦ When prices are rising but volume falling, the uptrend is losing momentum, and is maybe near the end. The price rise will slow and possibly reverse.

♦ When prices are falling and the volume increasing, prices will continue to fall, the downtrend will persist.

♦ When prices are falling and volume decreasing, the downtrend is losing momentum and maybe near the end.

♦ Volume tends to expand rapidly as prices reach a major high. And when the market takes a longer time to form a bottom, the volume is usually low for an extended period.

Open Interest

The technician's guidelines for assessing open interest are:

♦ Increased open interest means money is flowing into the market.

♦ Decreased open interest means money is flowing out of the market

Technicians believe open interest in the derivatives markets can tell you the following:

♦ Increased open interest, when prices are rising, indicates new buying.

◆ Decreased open interest when prices are falling suggests short positions are liquidating. Prices are advancing on short covering, not new buying.

◆ When prices are falling, an increase in open interest indicates short hedging and short selling. This signals the downtrend will persist.

◆ Falling prices with declining open interest implies long positions are liquidating which hints that the downtrend is losing the strength to continue.

If volume and open interest are both increasing, the current price trend will probably continue in its present direction (either up or down). If, however, volume and open interest are declining, the action can be viewed as a sign that the current price trend may be ending.

COMPUTERISED TRADING METHODS

Technical analysis relies heavily on charts, various indicators and statistics, but how all this data is interpreted normally depends on fallible human judgement, often heavily influenced by emotions of greed and hope, etc. Computerised trading systems were devised to remove the human element.

Trading programmes mathematically generate trading signals which indicate when to buy and sell, enabling you to avoid the agony of making decisions. Such programs are based on a variety of statistical indicators.

Two of the most common are moving averages and oscillators.

Moving Averages

Technicians see moving averages as one of the most versatile and widely used of all computerised technical indicators. As the name suggests, a moving average is an average of a changing body of data.

A 10-day moving average, for example, is obtained by

adding prices for the last 10 days and dividing by 10.

The term "moving" is used because only the last 10 days' prices are used in the calculation. Therefore, the body of data to be averaged moves forward with each new trading day.

Essentially, the moving average is a levelling-out device. By averaging the price data, high and low prices are obscured and the basic underlying trend of the market is more easily discerned. By its very nature, however, the moving average line lags behind the market action.

A shorter moving average, for example a five-day one, would hug the price action more closely than a 40-day moving average. Shorter-term averages are more sensitive to price action, while longer-range averages are less sensitive.

Technicians use one or two moving averages:

◆ *Using One Moving Average*

When the closing price moves above the moving average, a buy signal is generated. Conversely a sell signal is given when the closing price falls below the moving average.

For further reassurance, traders like to see the moving average line itself turn in the direction of the price crossing. Figure 17 illustrates the use of one moving average.

Figure 17
Trading system using one
moving average

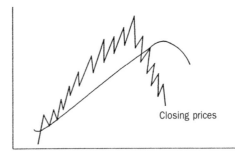

Closing prices

◆ *Using Two Moving Averages*

When two moving averages are employed, the longer one is used for trend identification and the shorter one for timing purposes. The interplay between the two averages and the price produces the trend signals.

A buy signal arises when the shorter average (a 5-day average) crosses above the longer (20-day) average. A sell signal is given when the shorter crosses below the longer.

However, because moving averages by nature are trend-following, technicians believe they work best when markets are in a trending period. They are thought to perform poorly when markets get choppy and trade sideways for a period of time.

Buy and sell signals are given by the crossing of the two moving averages. A buy signal occurs when the shorter line crosses below the slower line.

Oscillators

When a price oscillates between two price levels most trend-following systems are seen to not work well. The technician sees the oscillator as a tool to help him profit from markets moving sideways and from trendless markets.

Some oscillators have a mid-point value which divides the horizontal range into two halves, an upper and a lower. Depending on the formula used, this mid-point is usually a zero line. Some oscillators have upper and lower boundaries ranging from 0 to 100 or -1 to +1, depending on the way they are constructed.

Oscillators are used to identify "overbought" or "oversold" market conditions. A market is said to be overbought when it is near the upper extreme and oversold when it is near the lower boundary. This is a warning that the price is overextended and vulnerable.

The crossing of the zero line is often used to generate buy and sell signals. A crossing above the zero line would be a buy signal, and a crossing below this line a sell signal. Buy positions should only be taken on crossing above the zero line if the market trend is up. Short positions should be taken on crossings below the zero line only if the price trend is down (see Fig. 18).

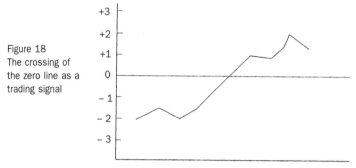

Figure 18
The crossing of
the zero line as a
trading signal

Technicians claim that oscillators can also signal that a trend may be ending by displaying certain divergences — that is when the oscillator line and price line diverge from one another and start to move in opposite directions.

In an uptrend prices may continue to rise but the oscillator fails to confirm the price move into new highs. Technicians see this as an excellent warning of a possible rally failure and is called a bearish or negative divergence.

In a down-trend, if the oscillator fails to confirm the new low move in prices, a positive or bullish divergence exists and warns of at least a near-term bounce (Fig. 19).

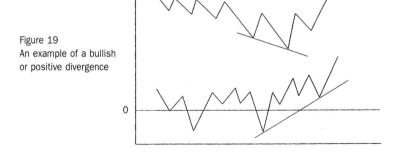

Figure 19
An example of a bullish
or positive divergence

There are several types of oscillators used by technicians.

◆ *The Relative Strength Index (RSI)*

Technicians believe the RSI indicates whether the market is over-bought or over-sold. When the RSI is 70 and above, they call this an over-bought situation and contend the price will soon turn down. Similarly, when the RSI shows 30 or lower, an oversold situation is said to have occurred and the market will be correcting upward.

◆ *Stochastics*

These differ from the RSI in that they often range between the extreme of zero (signifying extreme price weakness) and 100 (extreme price strength). High stochastics are seen as a sell signal while low stochastics act as a buy signal.

◆ *Moving Average Convergence and Divergence (MACD)*

When this crosses from below to above the zero line, technicians see this as a signal to buy. A cross-over of the MACD from above to below the zero line is a sell signal.

The MACD is also used to detect divergences or convergences. Divergences occur when prices make new highs, but the MACD fails to record corresponding higher peaks. Convergences occur when prices drop to successive lows, but the MACD does not show lower bottoms.

Technical Analysis Analysed

Many Singapore and Malaysian traders follow the principles of technical analysis. For some it is almost an article of faith and they avidly read all the available literature and, on occasion, attend expensive seminars overseas to keep abreast of the latest developments. Numerous books on technical analysis are also widely available locally.

But since the early 1960s a rising tide of critical studies have questioned the foundations of technical analysis as well as its claimed success rate.

These studies found their origin in the Random Walk Model first described by a French mathematician Louis Bachelor in 1904. He studied the fluctuations in commodity prices and found price movements were random. He discovered past price data was of no help in predicting future price movements.

His work lay dormant for 60 years until other researchers began to study share price movements. Wall Street analyst David Dreman in his book "Psychology and the Stock Market" has thoroughly studied the claims of technical analysis and describes the many research projects made to assess its accuracy as a forecaster of prices.

He reports one early work as showing that randomly chosen series of numbers, when plotted together, resembled actual charts of a share's price movements over a period of time. Another study showed share price fluctuations were remarkably similar to the random movements of minute solid particles suspended in fluids and known as "Brownian Motion", after the Scottish botanical explorer Robert Brown, who first observed this activity in 1827.

A number of detailed studies have "demonstrated that stock movements were random, that the proof of trend vital to the technician could not be found," Dreman notes. One study analysed the prices of 30 stocks in the Dow Jones Industrial Average at varying time intervals (between one day and two weeks) for more than five years. His results firmly supported the Random Walk hypothesis.

In another study cited, a computer analysed 548 stocks trading on the New York Stock Exchange for a five-year period. The price fluctuations were scanned to identify any one of the 32 most commonly followed patterns, including head and shoulders and triple tops and bottoms. It was programmed to act on its findings as a technician would. For example, it would buy an upside breakout after a triple top or sell after the market had plunged through the support level of a triple bottom.

The computer measured its results, based on these signals, against the performance of the general market. There seemed to be no correlation between the buy and sell signals and subsequent price movements. Traders who had bought and held shares during these periods, rather than constantly buying and selling them as the technical approach would have dictated, would have done as well.

Price-volume systems met with the same fate. Neither the size of the price nor volume changes appeared to influence price trends or the magnitude of their fluctuations.

Shares going down on heavy trading were just as likely to reverse themselves and rise in the next period as were shares currently going up on large volume.

Technicians claim their methods work and the examples they cite certainly appear to prove this. But their success is only in accordance with the law of averages. Even a trader who randomly selects securities or commodities will experience a certain degree of success. Moreover, technicians being human will forget their "misses" and remember their "hits". If they are wrong they will claim it was not the basic technique but its misapplication or contend that another application or supplementary information was required.

Technicians also argue that some systems have worked over certain periods of time, and cite computer evidence to support their claims. But when their results were tested more thoroughly, using different time periods and more extensive price information, the correlation quickly disappeared, again showing the systems were based on chance. The tests all indicated that mechanical rules do not result in returns any better than the simple hold-and-buy strategy. Evidence refuting the technical approach is vast and appears to strongly support the Random Walk hypothesis. Though some tests have shown that slight dependence (a small correlation between past and present prices), does occur it is insufficient for traders to profit from. Any small profit generated by use of such correlations is absorbed by brokers' commissions.

In the light of the above evidence Dreman concludes that:
"If stock prices are random, then no matter what price and volume information you have or how strong a chart may look, it is meaningless as a predictive instrument. The next move is entirely **independent** of the preceding one. If the stock has moved up seven days in a row, this has no influence on the eighth. It can trade up or down or be unchanged, just as a coin coming up heads many times in a row has a 50-50 chance of coming up heads again on the next toss."

Variations on a Theme

Technical analysis takes many forms. Two of the best-known are Japanese Candlesticks and Elliott Waves.

Japanese Candlesticks

The former is little more than a rather picturesque Japanese version of technical analysis. The difference is cosmetic. Whereas technicians chart price movements with plain vertical lines, the candlestick practitioners depict them with little candles.

Though visually cute this method works on the same principles as technical analysis. Its results are likely to be equally depressing for its practitioners.

Elliott Waves

The Elliott Wave principle was developed in the 1930s by R. N. Elliott and sees a bull market rising with a series of five waves (three upwaves and two corrective down-waves) followed by a market downtrend with three waves (two down-waves and one up-wave). The eight waves together constitute a cycle. Then there is a super-cycle which covers successive cycles that show a general upward or downward trend. Finally, Millennium Cycles which are made up of eight supercycles.

Economic events also appear to have a cyclical regularity: boom is followed by bust and then another recovery leading to a new boom. Inflation gives way to deflation and then re-asserts itself. When a commodity's price rises too high, consumption of the commodity is reduced, leading to lower prices cheap enough to stimulate consumption again.

"Elliottologists" claim that these economic cycles are sufficiently regular to profit from. The Elliott Wave will indicate when a market cycle is down and when it has reached a peak, so telling investors when to buy and sell.

Unfortunately for Elliottologists the cycles they talk about are always irregular in duration and intensity, having little of the predictability of those in nature.

For example the so-called business cycles vary enormously in time. In the US there have been seven business cycles recorded by the National Bureau of Economic Research from May 1954 till July 1981. From trough to trough their duration was: 47 months, 34 months, 17 months, 52 months, 64 months and 28 months.

Moreover, the business cycle that started in November 1982 saw a five-year bull market to the October 1987 crash, and a quick resumption of the bull market.

Thus while cycles can be found in economic activity as well as in nature, those in the former are far more erratic and difficult to predict. There is a vast difference between changing seasons and changes in human behaviour, especially in how it manifests itself in the investment markets.

Other technical trading methods include Fibonnacci numbers, Gann Waves, Kondratiev Cycles and Dow Theory. But there is not the space to discuss them here, except to say they display similar weaknesses to the aforementioned systems.

Despite the adverse academic findings on technical analysis and related systems, they continue to flourish. People pay hundreds of dollars to buy newsletters and books detailing the latest systems that technicians and their ilk have produced. Technicians disregard these findings — if they are aware of them — because they claim "their" system is different, and hope their clients also ignore the research. But for many investors the blandishments of technical analysis had begun to pall by the early 1960s. They started to pay attention to what seemed a much sounder method for assessing investments — fundamental analysis, the subject of the next chapter.

Useful References

"Psychology and the Stock Market," *by David Dreman*
"A Random Walk Down Wall Street," *by Burton G. Malkiel*
"Trading Asia-Pacific Financial Futures Markets," *by Will Slayter and Edna Carew*
"How the Best-Laid Investment Plans Usually Go Wrong," *by Harry Browne*
"How to Invest in Commodities, Gold and Currencies," *by Doreen Soh*
"Investment Management" *by Saw Swee-Hock*

CHAPTER ELEVEN

Fundamental Analysis

D iscovering the "true" worth of an investment is the professed aim of fundamental analysis. This approach assumes all investments have inherent determinable values which are often incorrectly appraised by the market. By locating and buying into investments below their true value an investor will make a profit when the market realises its mistake and starts pushing up prices, say fundamentalists.

This type of fundamental approach is prevalent in share markets. It began to be widely used from the early 1960s on Wall Street. It took over from technical analysis when the latter's deficiencies became obrious.

Fundamental analysis is now the preferred approach for most security analysts. One of its central procedures is the "top-down" approach where first the overall economy, then industries and finally individual companies are analysed. This sequence of analysis for shares was described in Chapter Two.

What is Fundamental Analysis?

How you define fundamental analysis depends firstly on whether securities or other types of investments are being assessed.

Securities

Fundamental analysis is most often associated with analysing securities values, especially shares, and follows specific procedures, the chief of which is forecasting a company's future earnings. Fundamentalists see growth in earnings and therefore the ability to pay dividends as the key element in estimating the intrinsic or what is often called the "firm foundation" value of a share or stock. A proven record of past performance in earnings growth is regarded as a reliable indicator of future earnings growth. Hence fundamentalists place great emphasis on such measurements as the PE ratio.

~~ YE SHALL BELIEVE IN THE P/E RATIO BEFORE ALL ELSE

The PE ratio is of key concern to all fundamentalists.

The quality of the company's management team is also assessed. If an efficient management team is running a company it is likely to keep achieving good results.

Company assessments are complemented with surveys of the company's industry and the overall state of the economy.

With fixed-interest investments, such as company bonds, a company's earning capacity and ability to pay interest on its loans would be the key concern. However, interest rate trends would also be central to any calculations by fundamentalists because fluctuations in interest rates will affect bond yields.

With securities the fundamentalist believes the supply and demand for a security, and therefore its price, will ultimately depend on investors correctly perceiving its long-term earning potential. The readiness by investors to buy and sell it will be based on a "correct" perception of its value. Its price will then rise or fall accordingly.

Other Investments

When fundamental analysis is applied to such investments as commodities, gold or financial instruments, a much broader range of supply/demand factors are considered.

The National Futures Association in the US defines fundamental analysis as: "The study of basic, underlying factors which will affect the supply and demand and hence the price of a futures contract."

Here, factors being considered are those that dictate the consumption (requirement for) or production (availability of) an asset. Because a non-securities asset does not produce earnings, there would be no investors' perceptions of what its future earnings would be to influence its price. Instead the supply and demand for commodities, for example, would reflect consumer and industrial requirements. For agricultural and mineral products the existing stocks, production and usage, as well as industry demand, retail sales and inventories, are critical fundamental factors. To a lesser extent this is true for gold, but as discussed in Chapter Seven, a range of bullish and bearish factors, apart from production/consumption, affect supply and demand for gold.

With currencies, supply and demand factors are those generated by balance of trade, interest rates, growth rates, inflation, government policies and political factors, capital outflows and inflows, interest rate differentials, productivity and tourism, as well as the fickle speculative mood changes of the forex markets.

With interest rates, the key supply/demand factors are overall growth, inflation, spending levels and unemployment and government monetary policies.

We thus have two conceptions of fundamental analysis. There is one version used for securities where PE ratios and other measurements of present and future earnings are seen as key factors determining prices. Then there is another version which is applied to the currency, commodities and other markets and reflects the operation of supply and demand factors on prices, particularly those relating to production, consumption, availability and uses for such assets. But the type of fundamental analysis used to analyse shares and other securities is the one that has much received critical attention and has been found to possess serious weaknesses like technical analysis.

Fundamental Failings

Once again the academics began their assault by looking at the performance of the fundamentalist approach in the share market. The method's use of past earnings as a forecast of future growth trends was examined first. Oxford professor I.M.D. Little, in an article titled "Higgledly Piggledly Growth", concluded the recent course of a company's earnings was of no use in predicting future trends. He found that earnings growth, as did stock prices, appeared to follow a random walk.

Researchers in the United States conducted tests to determine the applicability of Little's findings to the US. Dreman reports their conclusions were similar. Changes in the earnings of American companies appeared to follow a random walk — there was no predictable pattern in earnings — from one time period to the next. One study examined the percentage change in earnings for 700 industrial companies between 1945 and 1964. The direction of year-to-year earnings did not continue, and actually showed a slight tendency to reverse itself.

For every company with years of rising earnings there were dozens of companies which appeared to be growth companies and had consistently good results for years (sometimes by loose accounting) but had subsequently collapsed. Dreman notes that, "...one of the vital tools of fundamental analysis — the ability to correctly predict future earnings — is based to a significant degree on the continuation of past earnings trends, with only random chance that past trends will persist."

The most telling evidence against the success of fundamental analysis comes from examining the record of investment professionals, most of whom apply fundamentalist techniques (often supplemented with some technical analysis) in their forecasts.

Wall Street analyst Goodspeed reports that from 1967 till 1982 only 31 per cent of professional money managers had performed as well as or better than the share market averages. "The pros are not beating the market; it is beating them!" he remarked.

Fundamental Weaknesses

Several reasons are usually given for the failings of fundamental analysis. They centre around the reliability of the data, the ability of fundamentalists to interpret it accurately and the effect of random events.

Data Problems

There are several problems with the data used for investment analysis.

◆ *Dated Data*

Company data and other statistics that fundamentalists so love to analyse lag behind reality. For example, company reports are usually six months out of date when they appear. The state of the company could have considerably changed during that time.

◆ *Missing or Incomplete Data*

Managements can often conceal bad news about their

company, which if known could give a less rosy view of its prospects and potential.

Difficulties in acquiring the relevant data is also a problem for commodities traders. You need to get information on a global basis with most commodities. But many countries from which you need vital information will be uncooperative. The developed countries will only provide information that suits them. If they are buyers they will issue inflated figures showing they have more of a given commodity than they actually do. This will keep that commodity's price down.

Conversely, producing countries, especially the less developed ones, understate their production to drive prices up. Again they are often so "statistically underdeveloped" that they do not have the organisational infrastructure to gather, process and evaluate information on their crops or other primary products.

◆ Too Much Data

The volume of data analysed by fundamentalists is formidable. Their desks are often stacked with research reports. "On Monday morning, these stacks often run two feet high!," notes Goodspeed. "One portfolio manager keeps up with the over-load by keeping two full-size trash baskets in his office."

With so much data to process and analyse many investment analysts suffer from information overload, greatly impeding their ability to make intelligent investment decisions.

◆ Narrow Data Bases

Fundamental analysts tend to specialise in one industry, or one type of investment, and so are surprised by events that occur outside their focus. Specific industries can be affected by developments in other industries and sectors of the economy.

For example, the Swiss watch industry was ambushed by developments in the semi-conductor field. The poor predictions of analysts may be as much due to factors they have ignored as well as those they have assessed.

Groupthink

Because fundamental analysts look at the same statistics and company reports, talk to the same corporate managers and to each other, and use the same analytic procedures they usually arrive at the same conclusions. They get lulled into making consensus forecasts through such groupthink and the desire to conform. And if they are also analysing faulty, incomplete or inaccurate data, their investment forecasts will suffer.

Unexpected Events

Any number of unexpected events can suddenly affect the value of an investment, whether at a company, industry or national level. The CEO of a company could die, strikes and industrial stoppages could affect a whole industry and on the international level crises and wars throw markets into turmoil, usually causing share prices to fluctuate wildly whatever their earnings projections might be. The Kuwait invasion of August 1990 demonstrated the effect of such events on investment markets.

Despite these criticisms the essential rationale of fundamental analysis is sound. Factors that fundamentalists study do dictate prices. But the problems are three-fold. First, the data is often incomplete, inadequate or, out-of-date. Second, various factors can distort a fundamentalists thinking, including the influence of groupthink and the narrowness of data. Third, unexpected events can upset his calculations.

Fundamentalists could be expected to produce better predictions if these obstacles were removed. If all the known data about an investment was accurate and comprehensive and if it was being interpreted in a competent and astute fashion one would expect the success rate to be higher.

However, over the last two decades another theory of investment analysis — the Efficient Market Hypothesis — has rejected this view. The EMH claims that no matter how accurate and complete the data and how well it is analysed, mediocre results can still occur, as the next chapter will explain.

Useful References

"Psychology and the Stock Market" by *David N. Dreman*
"The Tao Jones Averages" by *Bennett W. Goodspeed*
"All About Futures" by *Thomas McCafferty and Russell Wasendorf*

CHAPTER TWELVE

. . . .

The Efficient Market Hypothesis

No one can beat the market, no matter how smart or knowledge able they are. This is the claim of the Efficient Market Hypothesis (EMH) in its strongest form. News affecting investment markets is being constantly analysed and quickly acted upon by millions of investors, both professional and amateur, and is therefore immediately reflected in the market prices. In other words the market is so efficient at responding to news that no one can consistently buy or sell rapidly enough to beat the rest.

In explaining the theory Dreman says:

"The market adjusts to new information very quickly, if not instantaneously. Since important news events, both for the market as a whole and for individual companies, enter the market unpre dictably, prices react in a random manner. This is the real reason why charting and other technical schemes cannot work."

EMH comes in three forms — weak, semi-strong and strong, with each having its supporters.

The weak form rests on the Random Walk theory which states, as Chapter 10 showed, that past prices are useless in predicting future price movements. Successive prices are independent of each other. Past prices can not affect future prices. No investors can build profitable trading systems based on past price movements and trading volumes and any seeming patterns that they display. No matter how much information an investor has about past prices he has no advantage over those who lack this information.

The semi-strong EMH goes one step further and claims that besides past price information, news (publicly available new information) about an investment is already reflected in its price. With shares, for example, public information would include statements of earnings, dividends, bonus, rights issues or purchases by large investors. The instantaneous nature of modern communications ensure the rapid dissemination of such information. Also, modern investment markets and their players have a highly-developed, sophisticated capacity to record, analyse and assimilate news and react to it instantly. Thus, semi-strong EMH supporters claim that it is difficult for any investors to get such news ahead of the pack and act on it before the market does.

Again the failings of fundamental analysis have lent support to the semi-strong view. As the previous chapter showed, investment analysts, usually the most proficient practitioners of fundamentalism, are beaten by the share market index about two thirds of the time. News is already instantly registered in the price. No amount of assiduous study or astute analysis by investment experts will uncover any under-priced bargains on the basis of public information or previous price movements.

The strong form of the EMH argues that ALL known information about an asset, whether public or not, including "inside" information is reflected in a security's price. Thus even corporate managers and directors who would have access to privileged information have no advantage over any other investors.

If the EMH in all three forms is true then the best that investors can do is adopt a simple "buy and hold" strategy, especially with long-term investments such as shares. Buying a randomly-selected group of shares or bonds and holding on to them would be as profitable as trying to select which securities would be the best buy. As Malkiel caustically notes in "A Random Walk Down Wall Street":

> "...throwing darts at the financial page will produce a portfolio that can be expected to do as well as any managed by professional security analysts."

Throwing darts at the finance pages is as good as any other way to pick investments, say some.

The long-term trends in most investment markets, especially the share market, show that a naive buy and hold strategy will eventually benefit investors. Though share prices plummet from time to time, Malkiel shows that for the 60 years on the US share market from 1930 to 1990 the overall gain has been 10 per cent a year, including dividends and capital gains.

The Singapore share market has shown a similar upward trend from January 1986 to December 1995 when the STI Index rose from 560 to 2050 — an average of 15 per cent a year for the 10 years.

Again in the US from 1968 to 1989 the compound annual rates of return on the following investments were:

Stocks   . . . .   10.0 per cent
Bonds 8.3
Forex 3.1
Gold 11.1
Silver 4.5

Malkiel also cites several studies performed on the records of professional investment managers using fundamental analysis. These studies show that randomly selected portfolios or unmanaged investments in stock indices investments do as well as or better than professionally managed portfolios. One study showed that from 1973-89, 70 per cent of the equity portfolios of pension-fund managers had been outperformed during this period by the Standard & Poor's 500-Stock Index. Over the entire period, an investor would have earned a cumulative return over 200 percentage points higher by investing in an index fund as opposed to a professionally managed fund, such as a unit trust. (An index fund buys all the shares in a given share index. No trading of securities is undertaken to try and beat the average. The return received by investors in such funds is that of the share index that a fund has invested in. For example, if there had been a STI index fund from January 1986 till December 1998, the gross return to the fund's investors would have been 15 per cent a year).

Certainly evidence indicates that markets studied in the US are highly efficient. When the professionals cannot outperform the broad market averages an efficient market is operating. It would seem that information is being quickly and widely dispersed and analysed by the whole market. Prices are immediately reflecting the new information, preventing any investor from gaining an advantage over others by getting in (or out) before prices have risen or fallen. But despite the EMH's convincing record weaknesses have been found in it.

EMH Analysed

Like technical and fundamental analysis EMH has been critically scrutinised in the last 20 years and been found defective in its semi-strong and strong forms. There forms are based on the assumption that all information is immediately absorbed and acted on by the market.

The EMH's weaknesses fall under the following headings:
♦ Information
♦ Market psychology

- Share market anomalies
- Insider trading

Information

The EMH rests heavily on the claim that news not only travels instantly, but that all relevant market players receive it at the same time, assimilate it with equal rapidity and draw the same conclusions from it. These are powerful assumptions to make even in today's world of instant communication, where hoards of investors have immediate access to latest market information.

As Malkiel notes: "I doubt there will ever be a time when all useful inside information is immediately disclosed to everybody." A possible exception might be large public companies. Because large institutional investors follow them closely, any news about such companies would be quickly reflected in their prices. But such is not likely to be so with the thousands of smaller companies not followed by the professionals. News about them would not always reach the market so quickly, nor be so thoroughly and uniformly assimilated by investors, institutional or otherwise.

Here the more astute investors who follow small companies could beat the market. They could buy (or sell) the shares in such companies before prices fully reflected the latest news about them.

Market Psychology

Even when all market participants receive the same news about an investment at the same time, there is no guarantee they will interpret it the same way or give equal weight to its importance.

During a bull market shares, for example, can be bid way above whatever fundamentalists think is their intrinsic value, often to ridiculous levels. The great tulip bulb craze of the 17th century, not to mention more recent share market and otherinvestment market frenzies, have demonstrated this. Investor hysteria was evident in the gold market by January 1980 when gold hit US$875 an ounce.

The market had gone mad.
Investors were seized by
gambling fever and the gold
price had ceased to even remotely
reflect whatever fundamentals
were pushing it up. As one
London gold dealer at the time
said, he expected gold to hit
US$1000 an ounce. Though it
was "good for business" he
admitted, "looked at objectively,
it's pretty horrifying. We're all
booking our beds in the looney
bin."

The same madness can afflict
bear markets, especially those
in free-fall. Panic abounds and
investment prices plunge way
below any rational estimate of
their value. The great crash of
October 1929 and the October
1987 crash showed this. In early
October 1987 the Dow Jones
average was about 2600. But on
October 19, the index has
fallen by over 500 points to 2100 and then to below 1800 by
October 31.

As Malkiel rightly asks:

Hysteria hits the gold
markets in January 1980.

"This is efficient? To many observers, such an event stretches
the credibility of the efficient-market beyond the breaking
point. Did the stock market really accurately reflect all relevant
information about individual stocks and the economy when it

sold at 2600 early in October? Had fundamental information about economic prospects of U.S. corporations changed that much in the following two weeks to justify a drop in share valuations of almost one-third?"

From such observations one could deduce that any news or developments affecting share prices (as well as other investment assets) can have widely different effects on prices, depending on the market mood. A piece of news that might push a share price up or down 5 per cent in "normal" times, could be magnified five times or more if the market is in the grip of gambling fever or panic.

Share Market Anomalies

Despite the claims of EMH supporters, there are several anomalies, particularly in share markets which cast doubt on their arguments. One relates to low PE ratios and the other to the operation of insider trading.

Supporters of the semi-strong school of EMH believe that all public information about a company is reflected in its share price. They are sceptical about the ability of fundamentalists to analyse a company's earnings and dividends and to find "undervalued" shares, which represent good value for investors. But here the much maligned fundamentalist may have the last laugh, at least with regard to low PEs already mentioned in Chapter Two, where shares with low PE ratios would eventually out-perform those with high PEs. They are usually shares that have yet to be discov-ered by the market so their prices and PEs will be low. Evidence suggests a portfolio of low PE shares will often produce above-average rates of return, which will also lift their prices, producing capital gains. And you would only locate such shares through the time-honoured methods of fundamental analysis.

Conversely, high PE stocks are often current favourites with the investment community. When a share's PE is high it means its earnings are only a tiny fraction of its current market price. This can occur when the company's shares have shot up, far out-pacing any growth in earnings. Fashionable shares which have become the flavour of the month often fall into this category. But they can quickly plunge in value when they have failed to live up to investors' high hopes for them. When this happens investors get hit, not only with lower or even no dividends, but with capital losses as well.

Insider Trading

The strong form of the EMH holds that the market is so efficient that even those with privileged inside information cannot beat it. But a commonly observed feature of share markets is that shares rise before the announcement of stock splits, dividend increases and merger moves. Consequently, insiders trading on such information can clearly profit before the announcement is made. While such trading is illegal, the fact that the market often at least partially anticipates the announcements suggest that it is possible to profit on the basis of privileged information.

We also know that corporate insiders typically do well when trading shares of their own companies. Shares purchased by insiders often outperform the shares in a randomly selected group. Moreover, selling by "knowledgeable" traders has often preceded significant price declines. Thus the strongest form of the EMH is clearly refuted.

But what is "insider trading"? The KLSE defines it as:
"...not only the purchase or sale of a company's securities but also the purchase or sale of puts, calls, or other options with respect to such securities. Such trading is deemed to be done by an insider whenever he has any beneficial interest, direct or indirect, in such securities or options, regardless of whether they are actually held in his name."

The KLSE includes "...tipping, or revealing inside information to outside individuals to enable such individuals to trade in the company's securities on the basis of undisclosed information."

Reputable stock exchanges around the world make strenuous efforts to control insider trading. Tightened rules on disclosure make time lags in the dissemination of new information much shorter than they have previously been. Of course, the more quickly information is disseminated to the public, the more closely the market, the harder it will be for investors to beat the market.

In Singapore, the SES has an on-going policy of ensuring as much corporate information as possible is disseminated to the investing public.

To this end the exchange has devised a Corporate Disclosure Policy Manual for listed companies on the types of information they must disclose and the procedures for doing this.

The Manual states that insiders should not trade on material information which is not known to the investing public. Insiders are defined as all people who come into possession of material insider information before its public release. Such people include stockholders, directors, officers, employees, outside attorneys, accountants, investment bankers, public relations advisers, advertising agencies, consultants and other independent contractors.

Also, husbands, wives, immediate families and those under the control of insiders can also be regarded as insiders.

The Manual warns insiders to refrain from trading on the release of material information till it has been released to the media in sufficient time to permit thorough public dissemination and evaluation.

KLSE policy on insider trading closely resembles the SES's. The KLSE defines insiders as those "...who come into possession of material, before its public release..." Such people include controlling shareholders, directors, officers and employees, and frequently also include outside attorneys, accountants, investment bankers, public relations advisors, advertising agencies, consultants and other independent contractors.

The husbands, wives, immediate families, and those under the control of insiders, may also be regarded as insiders. Where acquisitions or other negotiations are concerned, the above relationships apply to the other parties to the negotiations as well. Finally, for the purposes of the Exchange's disclosure policy, insiders include 'tippees' who come into possession of material inside information."

The KLSE guidelines recommend that insiders should wait at least 24 hours after general publication of a company announcement in "a national medium". Where publication is not so widespread the exchange recommends a minimum waiting period of 48 hours.

The more successful such measures are by the KLSE, SES and other exchanges to control insider trading the more a market's operations will conform to the EMH. Even so at the semi-strong level the EMH is amazingly efficient at rapidly incorporating public information into prices. Nonetheless, there are factors at work that obviously distort the workings of the EMH, especially psychological ones. The next chapter considers these.

Useful References

"Psychology and the Stock Market" *by David Dreman*
"A Random Walk Down Wall Street" *by Burton Malkiel*

CHAPTER THIRTEEN

Contrarian Approaches

" *A* thing is worth whatever someone wants to pay for it," goes an old Latin saying. Though somewhat cynical, this view illustrates the powerful effect psychology has on assessments of value. Market mood and emotion have always heavily influenced investors' behaviour. All investment approaches acknowledge this, though in the case of the fundamentalists somewhat grudgingly. According to Malkiel, fundamental analysts believe "...the market to be 90 percent logical and only 10 percent psychological". They believe that once investors have discovered an investment's true value they will act accordingly.

The technicians though, believe the reverse — that the markets are only 10 per cent logical and 90 per cent psychological. Through their graphs and charts technicians think that they can divine the mood of other players and so predict their trading moves. They see the investment game as one of anticipating how the other players will behave.

Like the technicians, Lord Keynes, the famous British economist, believed psychological factors were the main driving forces in the market. He too based his approach on calculating what other investors would do, but without the technician's complicated paraphenalia (and judging by his brilliant success in the 1930s stock market far more successful than any technician). As the Great Man remarked over 60 years ago:

> "Investment based on genuine long-term expectation is so difficult today as to be scarcely practicable. He who attempts it must surely lead more laborious days and run greater risks

than he who tries to guess better than the crowd how the crowd will behave..."

Keynes drew analogies between this strategy and his now famous example regarding the judging of a newspaper beauty contest. Here you have to select the six prettiest faces out of a hundred photographs, with the prize going to the person whose selections most nearly conform to those of the whole group. But the smartest players realise that their personal criteria of beauty may be irrelevant in determining the contest winner. Instead the best strategy is to pick those faces the other players are likely to fancy. But other smart players are doing the same thing. Eventually the optimal strategy, says Keynes, is to predict what the average opinion is likely to be about what the average opinion will be.

When applied to investment the strategy means a buyer is prepared to pay a certain price for an investment because he expects someone will want to buy it from him at a higher price. Any price will do as long as others are prepared to pay more. It is reasonable to pay three times more for something than its intrinsic worth, as long as you can find someone who will pay five times more. This theory, appropriately, is called the "Greater Fool Theory".

Keynes said the professional share investor should not waste time analysing the intrinsic values of investments to gain a long-term expectation of their prospects. Rather he prefers to predict what investments the crowd will select and which will be most susceptible to "castle-building". He then tries to beat the crowd by buying these investments first.

Castles in the Air

People's hopes and fears have always had a powerful effect on the investment markets — as the Dutch tulip bulb craze, the South Sea Bubble and more recent examples of investor madness have shown. Malkiel writes:

"Greed run amok has been an essential feature of every spectacular boom in history. In their frenzy for money market participants throw over firm foundations of value for the dubious but thrilling assumption that they too can make a killing by building castles in the air."

The castles in the air impulse describes the psychological process by which individuals build up expectations about an investment. Once an investment has captured people's imagination they will push its price to ridiculous heights, despite strong evidence to the contrary. As "Adam Smith" of The Money Game notes:

"...the 'image' that a company or stock presents helps its price, and can keep it up long after the rational factors of earnings and return on invested capital have begun to deteriorate."

Over the decades companies with exciting new products have captured investors' imagination, as the following examples will show. In 1955 General Electric announced that it had created exact duplicates of the diamond. The market was enchanted despite the fact that these diamonds were not suitable for sale as gems and could not be manufactured cheaply enough for industrial use. Within 24 hours GE shares total market value had increased by $400 million, which was then double the current world-wide diamond sales and six times the value of industrial diamond sales.

In the 1959-61 period the shares of companies marketing glamourous new technologies associated with space travel, transistors and optical scanners soared. At this time the traditional rule that shares should sell for 10 to 15 times earnings had been replaced by the belief that PE ratios of 50 to 100, especially for glamourous issues, were OK. Even well-established high-growth companies, such as IBM and Texas Instruments, sold at PEs over 80. (A year later their PE ratios had sunk to the 20s or 30s).

The hot high-technology issues of the early 1960s were duplicated in 1983 with the emergence of biotechnology. The biotech revolution was likened to that of the advent of the computer, with its "gene-splicing" techniques that promised uses ranging from cancer treatment, to growing hardier and more nutritious food. The boom in biotech stocks exceeded that of the hi-tech equities of the 1960s. While the latter had sold for 50 times earnings, some biotech stocks were selling at 50 times sales. However, from the mid-1980s to the late 1980s biotech stocks lost their glamour and most had dropped by three-quarters of their market value. Some biotech products had not been approved by the US Federal Drug Authority and others got bogged down in bitter patent fights.

Finally in 1988, Johnson and Johnson announced that its Retin-A, previously used for acne, could remove wrinkles. The market value of its shares jumped by $1.5 billion. At most the product was only projected to achieve sales of $150 to $200 million a year by 1990.

We can see that once an investment has gripped the public's imagination its price can be driven to dizzy heights. But when an investment is out of public favour its price will plummet way below whatever fundamentalist assessment of its "true worth" would be.

More recently the Contrarian approach, based on the castles in the air theory, has systematically formulated these insights into investment market psychology.

Going Against the Crowd

The essence of the Contrarian approach is to go against the crowd and not be carried away by its frenzies and enthusiasms. One of its chief advocates, Richard Band, says in his book "Contrary Investing for the 90s":

> "The best profits come from putting capital into ventures that most investors haven't heard of yet or are too afraid to touch. The principle works in any market; securities, real estate, commodities, collectibles and currencies."

The essence of the Contrarian approach is to go against the crowd.

SNIFF

But Contrarians sensibly warn against putting money into any unpopular investment, whose price is plunging. After all, if everyone else is losing their head then perhaps they know something you don't. Nonetheless, they claim you can be a successful Contrarian without any special expertise; just a commonsense ability to read the market mood and use simple reliable indicators.

Reading the Market Mood

The ability to read the market mood is the key to contrary investing. The market goes through moods, just like individuals. After all the market is composed of people. "The contrary investor is really an amateur psychologist who tries to identify the mood of the market — and profit from it," says Band. He traces the various moods a market passes through as it swings between bullish and bearish stages.

"A bull market begins to rise in a climate of fear. Later, as the market scores additional gains, fear recedes and an attitude of caution takes over in investors' minds. After prices have climbed substantially, investors start to forget the bad old days of the bear market. Confidence reigns. Finally, as prices reach a cyclical peak, euphoria sweeps the market. At the top, all but a handful of investors are convinced that the market will keep going up indefinitely.

On the way down, the same emotions predominate, but in reverse order: first euphoria, then confidence, then caution, then fear. At the bottom of the bear market, nearly everyone believes that prices will drop even further."

As such, the Contrarian strategy is to buy into fear and sell into euphoria (or greed). Though it sounds easy, in practice it can be quite difficult. Most people hate to stand alone and go against the crowd and stand by an opinion that most reject. Yet it's precisely when the pull of the crowd is strongest that the market makes its most dramatic reversals.

The influence of the crowd prevents people from thinking rationally. Emotions dominate their thinking. This is the state people are in during market peaks and bottoms. They think the prevailing trends will persist. At the peaks, most people think the market will continue to rise and at the bottom that it will keep falling. When the overwhelming majority of investors believe existing trends will continue a major market reversal is imminent.

As Band says:

"Typically, though not always, the size of the majority will be larger at an intermediate turning point than at a short-term peak or bottom. And the majority will usually be biggest, loudest and craziest at a primary turning point — the kind that occurs once every couple of years.

Contrarians do not argue that 'the majority is always wrong' (This is a common misconception). The majority is often right, especially about the primary turning point for many months at a time. However, the closer to a consensus, the more likely that the majority opinion is badly mistaken....A virtually unanimous, emotionally charged majority is almost certain to be wrong."

For example, only 17 per cent of investment advisors were bearish in August 1987, two months before the October crash, according to a poll conducted by Investors Intelligence. This investment newsletter from the US, which has been operating since 1959, concentrates mainly on the share market. It monitors 123 investment services and reports on the number of investment advisors who are bullish, bearish or looking for a market correction. This publication has also found that a reading above 60 per cent on its bearish scale has always marked the bottom of a primary bear market.

However, a Canadian investment newsletter, The Bank Credit Analyst, has found that bullish sentiment by advisors usually peaks a little before a bull market does. Conversely, bearish sentiment is strongest a bit before the market reaches a primary bottom. For example, bullish sentiment peaked in the Spring of 1987, before the Dow hit 2722 in August.

The BCA found that a bullish reading of 75 per cent or more accompanies a primary top in a strong bull market, a signal to Contrarian investors to get out of the market. Conversely, a 65 per cent or more bearish reading indicates a primary bottom and a green light for Contrarians to buy into the market.

For those tracking market sentiment in the commodities market the US newsletter Bullish Consensus scans 100 sources of professional commodity trading recommendations, including 30 market newsletters. The newsletter finds that bullish sentiment fluctuates between 30 and 70 per cent and contends that at 30 per cent an over-sold (time to enter the market) condition is developing and at 70 per cent an over-bought (time to exit the market) condition is imminent.

From the above data Band derives the following guidelines.

♦ If bullish sentiment is 80 per cent or more over a four-week period, this is a good time to sell

♦ But if the bullish consensus is 25 per cent or less, then the market is begging you to buy.

♦ Beware of any sharp swing in advisor sentiment not accompanied by an equally large movement in prices. If bullish sentiment climbs rapidly, but prices do not, then the prevailing down-trend in the market is still intact.

Measuring the Mood

Unless investors are prepared to subscribe to newsletters such as those mentioned above, they must construct their own indexes for measuring bullish and bearish sentiment.

Band suggests (tongue in cheek no doubt) that you select as many local publications as possible, "preferably written by advisers with a fondness for brash and flamboyant statements or by 'pure' technicians who believe that trendlines and charts tell all." But even so such advisers are most likely to be swept up by the emotions of the crowd and would best epitomise any bullish or bearish sentiments the financial community is currently expressing.

Also, he offers some rule-of-the-thumb signs that investment letter writers will give when the market is at a major bull or bear turning point.

An Imminent Bull Market

♦ Longtime bulls will suddenly turn bearish at the bottom and the bears will predict a further price drop of 20 to 40 per cent.

♦ Cautious bears will recommend short selling in the belief prices will go even lower.

♦ Despite low selling volume at the bottom, technicians will be looking for a "selling climax" or worrying about broken trendlines, violated moving averages and "downside confimation" at the bottom.

◆ Advisers will stress the benefits of timing the market and speculative in-and-out-trading.

An Imminent Bear Market

◆ Diehard bears will turn bullish at the top, while the bulls will make outrageously optimistic predictions.

◆ Technicians will cite heavy trading at the top as proof that the market will go higher. Those who use charts will insist all is well because the market (or some particular investments) are trading above their trendlines and moving averages and are climbing to new highs.

◆ Advisers will preach the values of a buy-and-hold strategy at the top and urge you to "sit tight".

But remember, following these guidelines will not relieve you of the burden of assessing the value of the investment itself. Contrary thinking still needs to be used with other methods of investment analysis to get the best results. Besides reading the market mood you need to look at the fundamental factors of an investment, including those of an economic and financial nature affecting it. You should also be able to give several sound well-thought-out reasons why a particular company, currency, commodity or interest rate will turn around. This means you still have to look at the fundamental factors that affect investment markets as a whole as well as specific patterns of factors that affect particular investments, especially shares. Doing this requires an integrated forecasting strategy, such as the one outlined in the next chapter.

Useful References

"Contrary Investing for the '90s" by Richard E. Band
"A Random Walk Down Wall Street" by Burton G. Malkiel

CHAPTER FOURTEEN

An Integrated Strategy

C learly there are no easy formulas for predicting investment market trends or prices. Technical analysis and related methods have yet to prove they can give investors a better than random chance of beating the market. Fundamental analysis, at least as it is currently practiced by investment professionals, also offers little better hope. But as Chapter Two showed there are specific sets of fundamental factors that can be usefully employed in the share market and will be reconsidered in this chapter.

The EMH says you cannot beat the market anyway, so the best approach is a simple buy and hold strategy where you are condemned to watch random forces dictate the price of your investments. Your only consolation is that if you have invested in shares you should get about 10 per cent return over the long haul and about 8 per cent if you put your money in bonds. However, investors should only adopt such strategies if they believe, as the EMH claims, they can not beat the market. But there is evidence that suggests investors can, at least the smart ones.

Then there is the Contrarian approach, which is essentially a set of techniques for reading the market mood and people's attitudes to particular stocks or other investments. This approach certainly has merit. It is based on people's commonsense ability to understand crowd behaviour rather than decipher masses of graphs and statistics that frequently fail to measure, let alone predict prices. Certainly Keynes and other astute investors have done this with considerable success.

When used with proven aspects of fundamental analysis, particularly the specific patterns or clusters of fundamental factors identified by such writers as Leeb, Dreman, Malkiel and Band, such an approach looks promising. Evidence indicates that investors who use such patterns can beat the market and disprove the EMH. By combining market psychology with these patterns investors can forge more successful forecasting strategies, especially for securities. The following outlines such a strategy.

Pulling It All Together

A forecasting strategy can aim to predict market trends as well as prices of particular investments. Thus it must first look at major factors affecting the whole market and then at specific factors determining the prices of particular investments such as shares, currencies, commodities or other assets. Again, both market-wide and specific factors are of two basic types — fundamental and psychological. This means that you can have market-wide fundamental and psychological factors and specific fundamental and psychological factors. All four categories are required for a comprehensive forecasting strategy.

MARKET-WIDE FACTORS

The market-wide factors, both fundamental and psychological, affect investment markets in various ways.

Fundamental

In Chapter Two we described macro factors affecting the share market. These were: GDP growth rates, inflation, interest rates, political factors and liquidity. However, as subsequent chapters showed, these factors also affect the currency, interest rate and stock indexes, gold and commodities markets. At the same time psychological factors, such as market mood and investors' capacity to build castles-in-the-air, also profoundly affect overall prices as well as prices for specific investments.

The challenge is to work out which combinations of these factors work best and in what markets. It is not enough to merely have a shopping list of factors which affect prices of an investment market. You need to know how they interact and how different factors work at different times and interact far more with some factors than with others. Then you can locate key sets of factors which have a much stronger effect than others on prices.

Leeb identified one such set of factors linking commodity prices with inflation and therefore interest rates. He showed how commodity prices provide an early warning system for inflation, which profoundly affects investors' expectations and eventually feeds through to the share market, causing it to rise or fall accordingly. When commodity prices rise so do the prices of other products and services, pushing up inflation. When inflation rises so do interest rates, which however can also be affected by high growth creating a demand for investment funds.

Commodity price rises
can be early warning
for inflation.

Discovery of such clusters of factors will help investors track and time a market and indicate when to buy or sell.

Psychological Factors

Even so, as the Contrarians have shown, the mood of the market can often distort the operation of fundamental factors. The euphoria/panic of runaway bull/bear markets can cause the investment community to abandon all notions of fundamental value and worth. At such times the wise investor should be timing his market entry or exits by closely monitoring the market mood, rather than looking at fundamentals. This would particularly be so when the market is at a fever pitch of a buying or selling frenzy. Band's Contrarian pointers described above would be useful for investors at such times.

SPECIFIC FACTORS

Most of the factors described below relate to shares and loan stocks. With shares one should look for low PE ratios and otherwise sound companies who are in difficulty. But as always psychological factors are also operating.

PE Ratios

As already mentioned companies with low PE ratios seem to be more profitable investment prospects than other shares. "The companies with the lowest P/E ratios in the market have consistently done better than other P/E groups in every study I have been able to locate," wrote Dreman in 1977.

This generalisation appears to have held true for two decades. Favourable events that the market did not anticipate often cause a company's earnings to resurge. "It is the constant tendency of the market to over-discount negative news and then pay handsomely in a reappraisal when this original assessment proved too gloomy," he notes.

Even so, Dreman and others have qualified this observation.

Shares are often trading at very low PEs because the market expects their future earnings to fall. And there may have been a permanent decline in a company's earnings power, which justifies the lower market evaluation. You need to be sure that this is not the case with the shares you are considering.

PE Ratios and Company Size

One way to deal with the above problem is to look for big companies with low PEs. While a decline in earnings power is often justified, other times it is not, contends Dreman, especially with large companies, which "...have amazing staying power".

The [low PE] strategy that would appear to be safest, from the results of the tests we have examined, is to buy very large companies at low PEs relative to the market," he suggests. An investor who therefore buys the low PE giants at a discount from the market will not only benefit through increased earnings, but will make capital gains if and when its fortunes improve.

Also, concentrating on big companies with low PEs is a strategy that should suit the less experienced investor. Not only do big corporations have less chance of failing completely, but also an improvement in their results is noticed more readily by the market than for medium-size or small companies. In addition, a major corporation with a long record is usually less subject to accounting gimmickry, which protects the less sophisticated investor.

In the US such a strategy would involve buying the lowest PEs on the Dow Jones Industrial Index (composed of 30 companies) or the S&P 500. In Singapore and Malaysia investors could start with the 30 companies composing the Straits Times Industrial Index or the 40 stocks of the Business Times Composite Index.

Distressed Companies

Many sound companies with impressive long-term growth records go through troubled periods because of such factors as weak management, technological change or regulatory problems. Some of these companies will end up bankrupt or be taken over. But most will pull through, often with a tough new CEO at the helm. Chrysler's dramatic revival under Lee Iococca is an example, with its price soaring by 400 per cent in 10 months.

"The one feature that all distressed companies share is that their stocks crash — 60, 70, 80 per cent or more. Investing in such companies after they have crashed can bring astonishing gains," notes Malkiel. For example, Toys "R" Us shares leapt 30 times in five years after the company emerged from bankruptcy in 1978. Again, Penn Central's stock quadrupled in four years after going through the fires of insolvency.

Lowell Miller, in his book "The Perfect Investment", provides some guidelines on selecting troubled (as opposed to bankrupt) companies which have strong recovery potential.

◆ The companies shares must have fallen to 20 per cent or less of their five-year high. For big companies, banks and utility stocks this figure should be 30 to 35 per cent.

◆ The stock, after the crash, should be selling for below book value per share. (Book value is what remains of a company's assets after all liabilities have been paid)

◆ There must be some "signs of life", such as dividends and earnings.

◆ Fad companies with obsolete products that were once the flavour of the month should be avoided.

◆ The post-crash price of the company's shares should be showing an upward trend.

Other plus factors Miller identifies that can show the company is on the mend include: a dividend increase, low

PE ratios, insider purchases of company stock and a strong or monopoly market for the company's products.

Insider Buying

This can be a short-cut method for selecting worthwhile shares if you do not have the time to research them thoroughly. Band has noticed that shares favoured by insiders usually rise twice as fast as the market during a general rise and fall twice as fast during a bear market.

But these share-buying strategies involve a degree of risk, which investors can reduce by buying a portfolio of shares. Most investment advisers suggest 15 to 20 shares spread over several industries, rather than one to ensure an adequate risk spread.

The above has been a forecasting strategy based on particular patterns of market-wide and specific factors which have indicated significant predictive capacity. Further investment research will probably unearth more in time. But what we have just described is a combined forecasting approach that should yield greater success for investors than other forecasting approaches can give. Even these strategies would still require a lot of data gathering and analysis by investors to yield success. But at least investors who did use it should be in the "right ballpark" when deciding what to buy and sell. Once having made their decisions though they have to implement them. The trading procedures by which they do this is the subject of the next section.

Useful References

"Psychology and the Stock Market" *by David Dreman*
"A Random Walk Down Wall Street" *by Burton Malkiel*
"Market Timing for the Nineties" *by Stephen Leeb*

3

Trading Strategies

*D*etermining your risk profile, choosing your market and deciding what forecasting method you will use are the first three tasks required of any investment strategy. The next task is to devise an appropriate trading strategy for yourself. This involves several steps:

- ◆ Understanding the mechanics of trading.
- ◆ Learning how to control the destructive effects of fear, greed, hope and other loss-inducing emotions which afflict investors.
- ◆ Developing an effective set of trading tactics to maximise your efficiency as a trader, which involves entering and exiting the market at the best price and practising effective capital management.

CHAPTER FIFTEEN

The Mechanics of Trading

*N*ow we come to the nuts and bolts of investment trading. Once investors have chosen their markets and the investments they want to trade they must learn the mechanics of trading. Whether it be securities, derivatives or the spot markets, there are six main aspects to trading.

♦ The trading mediums you plan to use. Will you trade through brokers, banks or Authorised Trading Centres (ATCs)?

♦ Trading accounts

♦ Margins required

♦ Type of contracts used

♦ Placing orders

♦ Commissions and other charges

How each operates in share and other investment markets differs widely, as this chapter shows.

Trading Mediums

There are a variety of mediums through which investments are traded. The most common are brokers or agents of some sort, though other mediums also exist.

SHARES

Stockbrokers are the main medium for trading shares and other securities. But in Singapore, investors can also trade scripless shares of Singapore companies through ATCs at banks and stockbroking firms. In addition, banks have custody nominee accounts through which people can trade. Such accounts permit banks to perform many of the tasks investors must fulfill.

But first we will look at using brokers and broking firms for share trading.

Brokers and Broking Firms

A broker is essentially an intermediary between buyer and seller. In investment markets, brokers usually work through a regulated institution such as a stock or futures exchange where they accept orders to buy and sell such investment assets as securities or derivatives contracts for clients. Brokers are either members of such exchanges, or are employed by, or represent those who are.

In the stock market there are three types of brokers — dealers, remisiers and stockbrokers.

♦ Dealers are employees of a stockbroking firm and receive a salary plus variable bonus

♦ Remisiers are self-employed operators attached to a broking firm. Their income is based on commissions from trade they handle. They rent a working space from the broking firm and pay a fee for using its administrative services.

♦ Stockbrokers are owners or directors of a stockbroking firm which is a member of a stock exchange.

Now that the days of open outcry trading are over at the SES and KLSE all trading is done on a computer system. This consists of computer trading terminals located in the offices of stockbroking firms which are linked to the exchange's central computer system.

But despite the transformation wrought by computers most shares and other securities are still traded through broking firms and brokers.

Choosing Your Firm

Such firms vary greatly in size, services offered and margins allowed.

Clients who consider themselves self-traders may only demand satisfactory personal service and financial integrity from brokers and if trading in derivatives or spot, the highest possible margins and lowest commissions.

However, other traders want brokers who give them sound market advice, information about listed companies and tips on when to buy and sell. When selecting a broking firm, you need first to satisfy yourself about its integrity and competence. You should ask the following questions before opening an account with any firm:

- What is the firm's capitalisation? The greater its capital, the more assurance you have of its financial soundness.
- Are customers' funds kept in a separate account? Such funds should be deposited in segregated bank accounts and a licensed brokerage firm must treat customers' deposits as separate from its own monies.
- What margins does the firm offer clients, based on pledging securities?
- Is there any limit to how often a customer can call for quotes?
- Are the order phones taped? The firm should record all orders for both your own and their protection. Any errors or misunderstandings in orders taken can be quickly resolved if phone conversations have been recorded.
- How effectively and quickly does the firm execute orders? They should be prompt and report back to you.
- How customer-oriented do you think the firm is? Will they go that extra mile for you?

Broking firms should be able to answer these questions. But to fully assure yourself about a firm you should also see whether there have been past, or current or pending actions, sanctions or complaints against it. In addition, check with the stock exchange to discover whether the firm is registered, and if so, on which exchanges.

Choosing Your Broker

Customers should use the same care in choosing a registered representative broker who will service his or her account as they would in selecting the firm. You should pick your broker as carefully as you do a lawyer, dentist or doctor and not merely go for one who has been designated "broker of the month", or who you have met in a hotel seminar room. Also, beware of high-pressure brokers using unusual sales tactics to get you to sign up.

Beware of high-pressure brokers who use unusual methods to make you sign up.

A good representative will serve you well when, besides placing orders, he provides the latest information and analyses, makes recommendations and is ready to advise you on your trades.

Authorised Trading Centres

ATCs were introduced in July 1994 to enable Singaporean investors to trade in scripless shares and rights to shares of Singapore listed companies. The ATCs set up at selected banks and stockbroking firms, permit investors to bypass the traditional method of trading through brokers at stockbroking firms. This new trading system was established in response to calls from small investors who found it difficult to be accepted as clients by stockbroking firms.

However, there are a few restrictions when trading at ATCs. For example, CPF funds cannot be used for transactions greater than $50,000 a day and all orders must be executed at the prevailing prices. ("Investing in Stocks and Shares" by Catherine Tay Swee Kian gives a detailed description of ATC trading)

Banks

A third way to trade in securities is through safe custody or nominee accounts with banks, which provide a one-stop service for investors. After buying a share, for example, an investor can open a safe custody account with his bank, instruct it to buy the shares, register them in his name and safe-keep them for him.

But investors can make it even easier for themselves by using a bank's nominee service. Here you can have all your shares registered in the name of the bank's nominee company. The bank will sign documents and collect dividends and bonus issues for you. It will also watch for announcements on rights and bonus issues and on general meetings called by a company and act according to your instructions.

In addition, the bank would have links with several broking firms and can obtain opinions from them for you on any securities you may want to sell. The bank can both buy and sell shares for you and credit or debit your account accordingly. Apart from normal brokerage fees, banks charge fees for these services.

The handling fee for each trade may be $10. Finally, investors who want to buy foreign shares, bonds, treasury bills and government stocks can do so through a bank's overseas branches.

DERIVATIVES AND SPOT TRADING

In the derivatives and spot markets trading is conducted by brokerages and broking firms in one form or another, whether through exchanges or on OTC networks.

In futures exchanges, such as SIMEX, trading is still by the open outcry method and executed by a variety of floor personnel. They include brokers who are floor traders employed by clearing, non-clearing or associate members of the exchange or individual members who trade on their own account. Also, there are floor account executives employed by the various types of members to relay orders from main offices of brokerage firms to floor traders. They follow through trades and keep the paperwork in order.

Guidelines to follow when choosing firms for derivatives and spot trading are similar to those for selecting share-broking firms. However, there are some extra questions to ask with the former.

♦ During what hours is the firm's order desk available?

♦ What commissions does the firm charge? Unlike share trading, commissions and fees for derivatives and spot trading vary widely from firm to firm. Moreover, you pay them on a "round turn" basis. With shares, charges are levied when shares are bought and again when sold.

Also, ensuring a firm is licensed is particularly important in futures trading where bucket shops abound, especially in the commodities sector. Once again, trading through a licensed member of an organised exchange, provides protection for traders. In futures exchanges, the clearing house, which clears and guarantee all trades, is central to these safeguards.

Firms are usually bucket shops if they are not clearing or non-clearing members of a futures exchange, though they may claim they are associate members of exchanges. But there is no way of knowing for sure. The best course of action is to ask an exchange for a list of their members and check to see which have branches or a parent company in the home city of the foreignexchange which is trading in the commodities or other investments that interest you.

Bucket shops in Singapore usually trade commodities on foreign exchanges. Another pitfall to avoid when trading in derivatives is not to give discretionary authority to a broker to trade on your behalf. Many responsible broking firms refuse to perform discretionary trading.

Investment professionals, like all experts, are there to guide and advise clients, not think for them.

Trading Accounts

Whether you want to trade in shares or derivatives you must open a trading account after choosing a broking firm and broker.

SHARES

When trading in shares in Singapore and Malaysia you must open two accounts with your broker. First a CDP account (in Singapore) or a CDS account (Malaysia) needs to be opened and second a trading or cash account to buy and sell shares.

CDP Account (Singapore)

A CDP account handles all settlements of sales and purchases or scripless shares, including crediting dividend payments and bonus issues from listed companies.

CDP accounts are of two types:

- **Direct Securities Account** - This allows investors to deal directly with the CDP, which sends them contract statements, confirmation notices, half-yearly and monthly statements of their shareholdings.

- **Sub Account** - Here investors are required to appoint a depository agent who can either be a member of the SES or a bank's nominee registered with the CDP. The agent is required to handle all settlements, including bonus issues, and to collect dividends and company reports for investors.

CDS Account (Malaysia)

Like a Singapore CDP, a CDS account uses the scripless book entry method to record transactions and keep track of shares, but does not credit dividends and payments.

Share Trading Accounts

A trading or cash account must be set up with an authorised broking firm in Singapore or Malaysia. The firm must either be an SES or KLSE member respectively. A trading account exists to record your shareholdings and current cash balance with brokers.

SPOT AND DERIVATIVES TRADING

With derivatives trading, such as futures, the setting up of trading accounts involves the following steps.

- A trading agreement is signed with the broking firm and specifies the responsibilities and obligations of each party, as well as the procedures to be followed in a dispute.

♦ A Risk Disclosure Statement is signed which warns the intending investor that trading is a speculative activity and they are responsible for all losses, including those that exceed funds deposited in an account. By such statements firms can cover themselves against clients who claim they were not aware of the risks involved in derivatives trading or that the firm did not warn them of such risks.

♦ The client makes a margin deposit with the firm (see margins below).

Margins

Margin accounts are central to derivatives and spot forex trading. But a form of margin trading is often used in the share market.

SPOT AND DERIVATIVES TRADING

With futures trading, margins that have to be deposited with brokerages range from 5 to 10 per cent of a contract's value. Similar margin requirements exist for spot market trading accounts on SIMEX or the OTC.

Margins are a prime concern for those trading in spot or derivatives markets, where a margin of 5 per cent can give traders enormous leverage and multiply both their profits and losses 20-fold.

For example, the margin required for a Loco–London gold lot is US$1500. If gold is selling at about US$390 an ounce, then a 100 oz Loco–London gold contract would be worth US$39,000, making the original US$1500 margin requirement about 5 per cent of the contract's total value.

Margins are set by futures exchanges as a fixed dollar amount per contract and have two components — Initial and Maintenance (or Variation) margins. The Initial margin is deposited with the broker (US$1500 in the above example) when the trading position is initiated. They are "good faith" deposits that investors must forward to their brokers to bind their performance on the contracts they undertake. Both long and short positions require margin deposits.

The Maintenance Margin is about 75 per cent of an Initial Margin. If the IM for a contract is $1500, then the MM would be about $1150. If the market moves against a trader to the extent that he loses $500 say, then his IM has been depleted by $500 and his MM by $50. When the latter starts being depleted he gets a margin call from his broker. The trader will then be required to promptly restore the margin, not merely to the $1150 Maintenance level, but to the Initial level of $1500.

Failure to respond to a margin call by brokers may result in them liquidating the position. Traders are therefore well-advised to check margin requirements with their brokers before entering positions. But margins can be revised up or down by exchanges depending on market volatility.

Also, margin changes can be retrospective and this may affect previously established positions. Thus a trader hanging on to a position with the minimum margin might be forced out of that position (forced to sell the contract and realise whatever losses he has made) if margins are unexpectedly increased.

SHARE TRADING

With share margin trading accounts you can use securities you already own as collateral to buy more shares. But not all shares are accepted as collateral. When you open a margin trading account with a bank or broking house you give your share certificates as collateral. The banker or broker will assess the quality and market value of the securities and lend you a percentage of the total. The margin given is usually about 150 per cent of the value of the collateral shares, while on fixed deposits it can be 300 per cent. But you will be charged interest on the money you use — similar to an overdraft.

If the value of the shares rise more money will be made available to you. But if they fall in value you will get a margin call, requiring you to deposit more money, sell some shares or deposit more share scrip as extra collateral.

Types of Contracts

Again, we must specify whether contracts for derivatives or share transactions are being discussed. Each type has a series of sub-types.

DERIVATIVES

There are three basic types of derivatives contracts — futures, options and forward contracts. Futures and options contracts are often speculative mediums which are standardised and can be traded on 5 to 10 per cent margins. Options contracts are similar in this regard though premiums rather than margins are used. But forward contracts are purely for hedging purposes and are fully paid. Also, their specifications are not standardised but tailored to suit individual requirements.

SHARES

In both Singapore and Malaysia ready contracts are used and contra trading is permitted. Before the advent of scripless trading immediate/cash contracts were also used, but are now redundant without physical scrip.

♦ **Ready Contracts** give investors up to eight calendar days to the trade date to pay for their shares.

If selling in Singapore, the shares will be debited from their CDP securities account on the seventh calendar day (transaction day plus - i.e. T + 7) while in Malaysia it will be T + 5.

Under SES rules shares must be paid for by 5pm on the day following the due date, or at the latest on 12.30pm the second market day (T + 7) after the due date.

In Malaysia, under the CDS, settlement is carried out on

T + 5. Sellers get paid by brokers on T + 6 and buyers must pay brokers by T + 7 (by 12.30pm) at the latest.

Contra trading is a form of trading on credit that takes advantage of the one-week (or longer) period given to make settlement.

In Singapore, the SES permits investors to buy shares without having to pay for them provided they sell them within a week, before the shares are transferred to their account. For example, if shares were bought or "contraed" on a Thursday then settlement would be due the following Thursday.

The KLSE however allows seven market days for settlement. Thus if shares were contraed on a Thursday then settlement would be due the following Monday week.

♦ **Immediate/Cash Contracts** existed when share trading was scrip-based. They required sellers to deliver their scrip on the same market day to their broker. Buyers would have to collect scrips and make payment on the following day after the contract. Such contracts were useful for those who wanted immediate cash for their shares. Sometimes the buyers would get a discounted price for the shares compared to those in the ready market.

Placing an Order

With shares, the normal board lot on the SES and KLSE is 1000. This means that all trades are in multiples of 1000. However, the SES allows some shares, such as those valued at over $10, to be bought in smaller parcels. The KLSE allows shares over M$15 to be traded in 200-share lots.

Odd lots, which can result from bonus or rights issues, can also be traded. But sellers must accept a lower price for them because brokers find odd lots inconvenient to trade. Conversely, if buying an odd lot to round up a lot to 1000, the buyer will usually pay more than the market price.

A range of trading orders exist to give investors flexibility in entering or leaving the market. The most common orders are:

The Market Order

Market orders are instructions to buy or sell futures contracts at the best possible price as soon as possible. This is usually preferable in:

- Fast market conditions, or
- When the trader wants to ensure that a position is taken and to protect against missing a potentially dynamic market move.

Stop Orders

A stop order specifies a price at which an order has to be executed. The following are examples of stop orders.

- **A buy stop order** is placed well above the market while a sell stop order is well below. For example:

    361.0 Buy Stop
    360.0 Market price
    359.0 Sell Stop

    A buy stop order is transformed into a market order by a trade or bid at the stop price. A buy stop order can be used to limit losses in a short position, or a buy stop can be placed above market resistance to initiate a long position on a bullish breakout.

- **A sell stop order**, placed below the current market price, is transformed into a market order by a trade or offer at the stop price. A sell stop can be used to limit losses on a long position. Otherwise a sell stop under support would activate a new short position or a bearish break-out.

    Thus stop orders can be used to establish a new position, limit a loss on an existing position, or protect a profit.

Limit Orders

Limit orders are used to buy or sell at a specified price or better. For example:

361.0 Sell limit

360.0 Market price

359.0 Buy limit

A **buy limit order** is placed below the current market price, and will be filled only at or below the limit price.

A **sell limit order** is placed above the current market price, and will be filled only at or above the limit price.

Stop Limit Orders

Stop limit orders are used like stop orders, but are restricted to the limit price, or better. They do not become market orders once the stop price has been reached. For example:

361.0 Buy stop limit

360.0 Market price

359.0 Sell stop limit

A **buy stop limit** is activated when an asset is bid or traded at or above the stop level. However, the order will NOT be filled unless the price subsequently drops to or below the limit price.

A **sell stop limit** is activated when the asset is offered or traded at or below the stop level. However, the order will NOT be filled unless the price subsequently rises to or goes above the limit level.

One Cancels the Other Order

This consists of two orders placed simultaneously. However, as soon as one order gets executed the other is cancelled. For example, the current gold futures price for December delivery might be US$395 an ounce. A trader who has a long contract might place the following one-cancels-the-other-order:

"Sell one December gold futures contract, US$400 limit and US$390 stop."

If the price of gold rises to US$400 an ounce, the long position is offset, profits are taken, and the US$390 stop order is cancelled. Alternatively, if gold's price declines to US$390 an ounce, the trader cuts his losses and the US$400 limit sell order is cancelled.

When buying or selling shares you give your broker the direction (buy or sell), the counter, quantity and one of the above orders. With futures contracts you need to provide the following information:

- Direction
- Number of contracts
- Delivery month and year
- Contract and, if necessary, exchange
- Type of order and any required price information
- Account number

Commissions and Other Charges

While commissions and charges for shares and other securities are fixed, those for futures and spot forex trading can vary widely from one broking firm to the next.

Securities

In both Singapore and Kuala Lumpur share commissions are on a sliding scale based on the value of the transaction.

Scales set by the SES for securities transactions on the Main Board and SESDAQ in Singapore are:

Value of transaction		Commission
First	$250,000	1%
Next	$250,000	0.9%
Next	$250,000	0.8%
Next	$250,000	0.7%
Next	$500,000	0.5%

Charges on transactions over $1.5 million are negotiable, subject to a minimum of 0.3 per cent. For contracts at prices below $1 a share special rates apply. The commission rates are $^1/_2$ cent per share for shares under 50 cents and 1 cent per share for those in the 50 to 99 cents range.

For non-convertible company loan stocks and debentures commission is 1 per cent on the first $50,000, 0.5 per cent for the next $50,000 and 0.25 per cent for the rest. The minimum commission charge is $5.

In addition to brokerage charges, other fees investors must pay include stamp duties and clearing fees.

In **Singapore**, these are:

- A contract stamp duty of 0.05% on the value of the contract.
- A transfer stamp duty of 0.05% on the contract's value.
- Clearing fee of 0.05 per cent of contract value to a maximum of $100.
- Goods and Services Tax (GST) of 3 per cent on commissions and clearing fees.

In **Malaysia**, these are:

- Brokerage rates (payable by buyers and sellers) for stocks, ordinary shares and preference shares.

Value of Transaction	Rate
First M$500,000	1%
Next M$500,000 to M$2 million	0.75%
Over M$2 million	0.5%

- Stamp duty — M$1 per M$1,000 worth of shares traded.
- Clearing fees are also 0.05 per cent of transacted value.

Futures Contracts

Fees charged for futures transactions fluctuate widely from one brokerage to the next. Commissions can range from about $25 to over $100, but most would be in the $50 to $60 range per round turn (the buying and selling of a contract).

In addition, exchange fees are about $1.20 per side of the contract. Also, with some derivatives such as stock indexes, fees of 7 to 15 cents are payable to the companies that collate them for every stock index contract traded.

Spot Market Transactions

The commission is added into the transaction price. For example, the spot forex buying price for the US dollar would be 1.4453 instead of 1.4450. But this 0.0003 of a cent commission would be for transactions of up to $1 million. For larger transactions it would drop to about 0.0002 of a cent.

Once you have chosen your broking firm and broker, made whatever margin deposits are required, signed the relevant agreements and familiarised yourself with contractual details you are ready to trade. But how effectively you do so will depend on how well you can control the emotions of greed, fear, hope and the herd instinct which afflicts even the most hardened market players from time to time.

Useful References

"How to Invest in Stocks and Shares" *by Robert Chia and Doreen Soh*
"Handbook for Stock Investors" *by Goh Kheng Chuan*
"How to Invest in Commodities, Gold & Currencies" *by Doreen Soh*
"Financial Markets and Institutions in Singapore" *by Tan Chwee Huat*
"Investing in Stocks and Shares" *by (Catherine) Tay Swee Kian*
"A Guide to Investment in Stocks and Shares" *by Wong Yee*

CHAPTER SIXTEEN

Keeping Your Cool

*A*ll investors, especially speculators, must control their emotions. Hope, fear, greed and the desire to follow the crowd will be strongest when the market action is fast and furious — the normal situation for speculators. But all investors can be adversely affected by these emotions.

Previously we considered psychological factors moving the markets. Now we will look at the psychological factors likely to affect you while trading. The key to managing the psychological aspects of trading is to understand the input of hope and fear, greed, pride and the herd instinct. Unchecked, these emotions spell ruin for even experienced traders.

Greed, fear, hope and pride etc
constantly stalk traders.

Hope and Fear

Traders are often betrayed by hope when the market turns against them. The more the price drops the more tenaciously they cling to the hope that it will turn in their favour. For them they need to follow the axiom, "When the ship starts to sink, don't pray. Jump". If they fail to do this and the price continues to drop their hope turns to despair and they exit from the market with a huge loss, swearing never to return.

Conversely, when the price goes in their favour, fear that the trend will reverse causes them to abandon their position before it develops to fruition.

Figure 20 below illustrates how damaging fear and hope can be to traders.

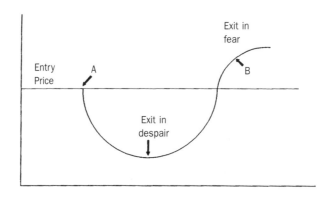

Figure 20

The wavy line represents market action. Markets do not travel in straight lines but undulate and work up to higher or down to lower prices. This movement adversely affects traders who lack strong self-discipline.

The horizontal line represents the entry level or the price at which the trade is established. If the trader enters at price A, hope keeps him in the market until it dips dramatically — he exits in despair at almost the lowest point. If the trader enters the market at point B and fear overcomes him, he will exit early and only make a small profit.

The same principle applies for traders who have taken short positions in the belief the market will fall. One need only turn the chart up side down, placing hope above the line and fear below it to see how hope and fear can undermine them.

Greed

Greed, though condemned as a vice since Biblical times, has, in recent years, been elevated to the status of virtue. One of greed's most recent exponents was jailed Wall Street financier Ivan Boesky, who coined the immortal phrase that "greed is good." This sentiment was popularised soon after by the reptilian Gordon Gekko, in the film "Wall Street".

It was resurrected in Singapore in 1993 by a Hongkong tycoon while he was addressing a receptive NUS audience of pre-university students and teachers.

Greed itself means wanting more than you originally sought or have a right to expect. It means losing control of your desire and breaking whatever rules, moral or financial, to satisfy its insatiable dictates. In the volatile world of investment markets, it constantly competes with fear and other emotions for control of the hearts and minds of all players.

It can manifest itself in various ways during trading. One is the urge to keep a position too long when it is rising. Greed makes you hang on for just a little bit longer, to achieve some goal — perhaps $10,000, $20,000 or $100,000 and so on. Your greed will not let you quit till you have achieved that magic figure. You may only achieve 90 per cent of it, but your greed will not let you stop till you have reached 100 per cent. So you keep riding. But then the price drops and you go over the falls and maybe lose the lot.

Even so traders may control their greed and get out with a profit, only to have the sickening experience of seeing the price soar after they have sold. This fear of regret that makes people stay greedy and refuse to let go after having already made a big profit. In fact one of Wall Street's famous sayings is "Never check the price of a stock you've sold." Thus learning to deal with the pain of regret is another must for trading success.

Pride

Traders, like most human beings, have an ego. They like to think that they can beat the market. Perhaps some, like Sherman, the bond salesman in "Bonfire of the Vanities," see themselves as a "Master of the Universe".

No trader wants to admit he has screwed up and made a bad trade. Refusal to admit they are wrong causes many traders to cling emotionally to positions reason has told them to abandon.

The Herd Instinct

Man is a social animal and likes to be part of the group. In fact society has conditioned him to want to conform and think the way the group does, and to feel uncomfortable if he does not. The desire to conform affects traders as much as anyone else. They fear bucking the market trend and the opinion of other traders. Hence the herd instinct normally triumphs. They follow the consensus even when they may have sound reasons for going against it.

You have to control your emotions to trade in a disciplined manner. Only when trades are dictated by a clear consistent strategy, rather than by fear, greed or hope can you hope to prevail in the markets. Control such emotions and you will develop the crucial virtues of patience and timing. They will give you the self-control to hold off if the market looks unpromising and wait for the right time to buy. Then you will not be needlessly risking your capital on anything that moves to still that speculative itch for action.

A set of sensible trading tactics will do much to help you keep a level head when playing the markets, as the next chapter will show.

Useful References

"The Zurich Axioms" by *Max Gunther*
"Why the Best-Laid Investment Plans Usually go Wrong"
by Harry Browne

Trading Tactics

A forecasting strategy tells you what investments to buy or sell, but trading tactics shows how to do this most efficiently. Central to trading tactics is market timing where the aim is to buy low and sell high. But minimising losses, calculating risk-reward ratios and making the best use of investment capital are also important considerations.

For speculators trading tactics are especially critical. They enter and exit from the market often and quickly; timing is particularly crucial for them. Speculators are under much more pressure than long-term investors to make quick and accurate decisions, especially when they are trading on big margins which permit them to trade 20 times their capital.

Volatile investments should be avoided by those with limited financial resources.

A small price move against speculators can push them out of the market, but the opposite can confer great wealth. Needless to say those with limited financial means should avoid leveraged speculation in volatile investments.

Because they are so vulnerable to price fluctuations the need to enter at the lowest possible price and exit at the best price is particularly pressing for speculators. For them a firm grasp of trading tactics is essential. And they should also keep Harry Browne's words in mind:

> "Any speculation can turn out to be a loser. No matter how careful your analysis, no matter how shrewd your system, no matter how favourable conditions seem to be, no matter how sure you are, the truth remains that anything can happen. There are no sure things in investing or speculating.

The key factor in any speculative strategy is the way in which the losses are allowed for, accepted, and limited — in other words, the way in which you control risk. You must have a way to keep any loss within acceptable limits. Trading tactics should thus start with loss limit strategies, then consider risk-reward measures, market timing (finding entry and exit points), efficient allocation of capital, and finally paper trading to get a feel for the market.

Limiting Losses

A loss limit is central to a profitable trading strategy. You must have a clearly-defined bail-out point — a specific price defined in advance to tell you when to get out and take your loss. And you should have a stop loss order in place to ensure you really do bail out at that point.

Once you buy an investment you are emotionally tied to it, blurring your objectivity, prompting you to put off selling for another day or week, while your losses grow. By deciding how much they are prepared to lose before buying, investors avoid this vexing situation. You need to clearly define what percentage loss in your trade denotes a signal to get out.

No speculative position should be open-ended, to be kept for however long it takes to succeed. This approach will immobilise capital for a long time, making it unavailable for more attractive alternatives.

Know your exit point with a trade before entering it. Without a predetermined exit point a trader is prone to procrastination when required to liquidate a losing position. Exit points will help automatically cut your losses.

Place a stop loss order when you make your order so you are not tempted to give the market a "few more cents" if the price of your investment drops.

A stop loss not only circumvents such emotions but automatically triggers the sale when your attention may be elsewhere. The price may be plunging and by the time you know what is happening the price may be several per cent below your bail-out point. But a stop loss is activated as soon as the price reaches that point.

Even so, place your stop loss orders with care because a stop placed too high (or too tight) can put you out of the market quickly with a loss if there is a slight price change. You can be "whipsawed" by poor placement of stops. The market may rise after you have sold and fall when you buy, putting you out of tune with it.

Again, a stop loss cannot over-rule a price gap — a sudden plunge in price, with no trades in between. Such gaps can occur between one day's closing and the next day's opening. If your stop loss falls between two prices, it will be executed at the lower.

The Risk-Reward Ratio

The gain you expect to make on an investment must be much greater than whatever loss you are prepared to sustain. While you may have fixed your bail-out point (with a matching stop loss order) 10 or 15 per cent lower than the current price, your expected gains should be many times greater. Calculating risk on share investments, for example, requires assessment of:

- Business Risk — How certain is a firm's ability to pay interest and dividends?
- Debt Risk — What debt burden does the firm have? How well can it service its loan?
- External Risk — How strong are the positive and negative factors beyond the firm's control such as the state of the industry the firm is in, and general macro-economic, political and social conditions affecting an economy.

For many players a worthwhile investment is one where the potential gain is simply greater than the potential loss. If, for example, the expected gain on a trade is $3 and loss $2 then it is a good bet. But after allowing for commissions, bid-ask spreads and ragged buying and selling executions, the potential gain may be much smaller than the potential loss. More than half such speculations must succeed for you to break even.

And remember: "Most successful traders have more defeats than victories. Success is achieved by making more money from the winners than is being given up by the losers — by letting the winners run up big profits while selling the losers quickly," says Browne.

You have to look for profits much greater than the losses you will inevitably experience. Bear in mind that losses can easily outnumber gains, so gains must be bigger than the losses. Also, profit estimate is usually little more than a guess. The investment might go up, but not by as much as you anticipate.

Thus a high risk-reward ratio is part of any speculative strategy. A ratio with a potential gain five or more times as large as the potential loss is recommended by Browne.

Finding such a high-profit prospect usually requires an investor to "go against the crowd" and adopt a Contrarian approach. The market usually offers only big odds when you view a prospect differently from most other investors. When you share the prevailing opinion, the price of the investment probably already reflects what you expect – leaving little room for profit even if things turn out exactly as you expected.

If you and everyone else is aware of an investment's potential there probably is little profit in it.

Market Timing

Knowing when to buy and sell is market timing.

Getting In

The price at which you buy will affect the potential loss and gain and the risk-reward ratio. Buying at the cheapest possible price is therefore important. But this not only means buying when you think an investment is cheap, but when its price has reached a point where it is unlikely to fall further. This is the entry or buy-in point for an investment. But how to identify such a point?

Browne recommends using the support and resistance concepts of technical analysis. At a support level technicians expect buying volume to increase sufficiently to stall or stop a price decline, while at a resistance level selling volume will be enough to stop prices rising. But Browne admits, "...they aren't always easy to find. In many cases, all your can see are many little jagged reversals in the trend, with no clear areas that have clearly stalled major price movements. Or the price may be a long distance from the nearest clear-cut support-resistance you can spot". Buy only when you have identified a clearly-defined support-resistance level. Otherwise, it is best to stay out of the market. Once you have spotted a support-resistance level the best place to put a stop loss is just beneath it – about 5 per cent below, though this depends on the volatility of the investment.

Though a trenchant critic of technical analysis, Browne concedes that some of its rules, "are grounded in the ways human beings act. These rules can help you make decisions concerning when to buy and sell." Support and resistance levels reflect not only the current mood of the market but the strength of the underlying factors. But it is important that you have some idea what these factors are if resistance and support levels are to be of any use.

Band suggests momentum (or velocity or rate of change) indicators could be used to identify promising entry points. He says:

"Momentum indicators are designed to tell you when a trend is slowing and therefore may soon be stopping. Unlike trend-following indicators, such as moving averages – which can only confirm a trend after the fact – momentum indicators can alert you to an impending trend change before it happens."

Essentially, momentum indicators compare an asset's current market price with its value at some point in the past. For example, if a share was $2 today and a week ago it was $2.20 then the rate of change is 10 per cent.

If in the next week the price falls 10c to $1.90 then the rate of decrease has slowed to about 4 per cent. When there is a slowing in a downward trend the price is starting to meet a resistance level, which is when an entry or buy-in point may be found. But again a clear awareness of how changes in the fundamental factors are affecting these indicators is important.

Getting Out

Taking profits is the next big test for traders. If your trade has risen in price you will have to sell at some point to take a profit. The question is, when? You may have set a target at which you will sell, but it may not be reached. And while you wait the price can drop from its peak. Or you might sell at your target only to forlornly watch prices go higher.

There is a way out of this dilemma — it is the Trailing Stop Loss. This is simply a stop loss order which is moved up as the price moves up. As the price rises you cancel the existing stop loss order and replace it with a new higher one. In other words the stop loss trails behind a rising price. For example, if you buy a share at $10 and place a stop loss at $9 and the share then rises to $12, you can raise the stop loss to $11. If the price retreats to $11 again the shares will be automatically sold, giving you a profit of 10 per cent. Conversely, if the share continues upward you can raise the stop-loss again and again - until the latest stop-loss is triggered by a price decline. Your investment would then be closed out at a substantial profit. The price may go still higher, but is less likely to do so after a major drop.

With a trailing stop loss you do not have to try and predict when your investment's price will peak. It is better to let your profits grow till the market says "sell" and triggers your stop loss.

Capital Management

The first law of speculation is to trade only with money you can afford to lose. If your are speculating with "the rent money", or funds needed for some other urgent purpose, you are setting yourself up for failure. Sound investment decisions are only made by a calm rational mind, not one driven by desperation, greed, or the need to make a quick buck to pay pressing bills. Your trading capital should be viewed as money you are prepared to lose, if necessary.

However, the amount of money you can spare for trading will determine what type of investments you trade in. With shares maybe only a few thousand dollars would be required. But with some derivatives, such as currency futures, where contracts are US$100,000 or more, something like $50,000 or more may be necessary. Much less and you will be trading by the seat of your pants on thin and very vulnerable margins. The slightest price dip could throw you out of the market, with not enough capital to get back in.

After deciding how much money you can afford to lose there are several other capital-management factors to consider.

♦ If you have a margin account ensure that you always deposit more than the minimum with your broker so that a small adverse market movement will not wipe out your stake, or force you to liquidate a promising position. This becomes agonising when the price of the liquidated contract then rises. Regular monitoring of one's margin and keeping a cushion of uncommitted funds can prevent premature liquidation.

With volatile commodities futures, for example, you should put up at least twice the required margin.

♦ Make sure that you do not bet too much of your capital on each trade. Obviously a few adverse trades will wipe you out if you allocate too much of your capital per trade. Bet half your capital and you will be eliminated far more quickly than if you bet only 10 per cent a time. The percentage of capital that one should allocate per trade will primarily depend on the volatility of the investment. The more volatile the investment the less money should be put on each time. Most derivatives, and specu lative gold and other mining stocks, and spot forex investments, belong to this category.

Paper Trading

Getting a feel for the market before you start trading can be a big help to novice traders. One of the best ways to do this is through paper trading. Doing "paper runs" first will help you refine and perfect your trading strategies before risking your money. Making investment decisions, calculating margins and daily equity, entering imaginary stop-loss orders on the sell side for long positions and imaginary buy-stops for short positions will sharpen your expertise. You will more efficiently implement trades when you start trading for real.

The above are five main elements of an effective trading strategy. But any strategy you devise will be enhanced by the following practices.

♦ When analysing a possible trade, work from the long-term to the short-term. See what the long-term price trends are before examining the latest price fluctuations. An upward or

You should test your strategies on paper first.

downward price trend for an investment may simply be a dip or bounce, against a long-term trend.

♦ Remember, "doing nothing" is also a trading option and should be considered when you see some weakness in a contemplated trade. Having to stay out of the game on such occasions will teach you self-discipline.

Much of the time markets show no particular trend, limiting any prospects for profits. Good buying or selling prospects come along only occasionally, so quell that speculative urge for action. You only generate commissions for your broker when you trade merely to keep your money in motion.

♦ Execute your trades promptly when a promising prospect appears or when it's time to exit. Fortune favours the bold and he who hesitates is lost.

Pitfalls

Apart from these specific procedures all traders, especially speculators should avoid the following pitfalls.

Avoid Being a Weathercock

Being a weather cock means you are constantly subject to others' opinions and will always be changing your mind. Once you have formed a basic opinion of the market (based on a thorough analysis of all the variables involved) do not let others sway you without sound cogent reasons or new and relevant information.

Excessive Averaging

Some traders resort to averaging when the market turns against them. For example, if the price of an asset has dropped they may buy more of it at the lower price to average out the loss of the original purchase. If you buy 1000 shares at $1 a share and they fall to 75c and you buy another 1000 then your total outlay is $1750 for 2000 shares, which comes to $87^{1}/_{2}$c a share. This means that you have averaged down your loss to $12^{1}/_{2}$c rather than 25c a share.

Though this may give you a certain comfort you should ask yourself why you did this. Are you buying the share because you genuinely think that there are sound logical reasons, or simply because the price has dropped? Are there improved fundamental factors or a more positive market perceptions of the investment that make it a better bet now than before? If not, you are merely kidding yourself with this tactic.

Refusing to Accept Losses

All traders lose sometimes, even the most successful. Losses are part of the business. But a refusal to accept losses can prompt you to hang on to a losing trade, rather than face the fact that you have taken a loss. When you accept losses and no longer suffer hurt pride when wrong the fear of defeat will have been reduced, making you a better and more resilient trader.

Riding Losses and Taking Small Profits

As already mentioned holding on to a losing trade is a deadly trading sin. The second is to compound this mistake by selling the investment as soon as its price recovers to show a small profit. People can be so relieved to get their money back, especially if they have also realised a small profit, that they dump the asset as soon as they can. (See Figure 20 in the previous chapter).

But a better strategy would be to resist temptation and hang on to the asset as its price rises (unless of course you have sound logical, as opposed to emotional reasons, for selling it).

Impulsive Trading

Do not trade impulsively. Always follow a plan. Decide on a basic course of action and do not let daily ups and downs deflect you. Constant chopping and changing will cause you to make hasty, ill-considered decisions that will eventually cost you. If the market is so volatile as to produce such indecisiveness then stay out till things calm down.

Excessive Transaction Costs

During times of frenzied trading, investors tend to forget that each trade carries transaction costs, an ever-present drain on trading capital. The larger such costs are as a percentage of trading capital, the smaller will be the chances for long-term success.

Not Knowing When to 'Take the Money and Run'

Sometimes you have been lucky enough to buy and see the price soar within perhaps 48 hours to yield a good profit.

In your emotionally buoyant state you may be spending more time wondering why the profit came so fast, instead of calculating when to get out. You should be making plans to exit (unless you have good reasons to think the price will rise further), rather than congratulating yourself on your good fortune. On such occasions the market favours those who take the money and run, rather than procrastinators.

The Kiasu Syndrome

The fear of missing out afflicts all traders, not only Singaporeans. This fear often prompts people to enter dubious trades rather than stay out of the market. They do not want the sickening experience of seeing the investment they have decided not to buy surge in price.

They would rather make a risky trade than risk experiencing kiasu chagrin for having missed out, if the price happens to rise. But ask yourself this: How many other times have you stayed out of an uncertain trade and saved money? When in doubt stay out.

Meeting Margin Calls

Traders who meet margin calls are usually throwing good money after bad. Never meet a margin call: if your position has deteriorated to that extent you should have pulled out long ago. Do not throw good money after bad. You have made a mistake. So swallow your pride, grit your teeth and take it on the chin like a professional trader.

Never meet a margin call.

Trading in Too Many Markets

Some traders trade on too many markets, making it difficult to focus their energies. It is hard to concentrate and analyse prospects properly if you are thinking about several markets and trades at once.

Here, you can not do the necessary homework required to make informed trading decisions, so reducing your success rate. As in war, concentration of forces is critical to success in investment trading.

Useful References

"Why the Best-Laid Investment Plans Usually go Wrong" *by Harry Browne*

"The Zurich Axioms" *by Max Gunther*

Conclusion

The investment markets are critical to the functioning of the global and national economies. The central role of such markets is to collect as much as possible of an economy's surplus wealth and re-allocate it to some productive use. The explicit hope is that this wealth is invested in areas most likely to benefit society.

But how well investment markets do this is a matter of constant debate. Occasional Barings, Daiwa and Sumitomo-type debacles indicate the task is often poorly performed when some investment market operatives act like gamblers with other people's money. As Keynes warned in 1935: "When the capital development of a country becomes a by-product of a casino, the job is likely to be ill-done."

However, ignorance allows such reckless behaviour to flourish. Investment market operatives are often disturbingly ill-informed about how the markets operate, as Leeson's comments about his superiors revealed. Such incompetence is probably rather more widespread among industry operatives than one cares to contemplate. Even so, the rapid proliferation of the scope and complexity of investment markets makes it difficult for even the most efficient operatives, let alone novice investors, to fully understand them. Clearer explanations of how markets operate would help remove the pall of ignorance that surrounds them. Present descriptions are often incomplete and inadequate, especially for the derivatives markets.

The initial aim of this book has been to describe the investment markets and their operations more clearly and comprehensively to new investors. But understanding the investment markets is only the first step to trading profitably. Knowing the rules of the game is one thing, playing it profitably is another.

Numerous forecasting methods claim to show investors how to do this. At first glance many look impressive, especially technical analysis and like systems. All those graphs and figures look so scientific. Again fundamental analysis, especially as practiced by investment professionals, looks reassuringly reliable in its quest to ascertain the "real value" of an investment. But studies over the last 30 odd years have proven that both these methods are seriously flawed and certainly no sure path to wealth.

The second aim of this book has been to show that while there is no instant formula for quick wealth in the investment markets there are promising approaches that can help diligent investors. It has summarised academic research over 40 years and has described patterns of factors that investors can use to their advantage.

Astute tracking of inflation and other macro-economic factors, detection of specific clusters of micro-economic factors plus, the psychological insights provided by the Contrarian approach, should at least put investors in the right ball-park when making investment decisions. To further help you make the most of your investment opportunities this book has described a range of trading tactics (often common sense) that should maximise gains and minimise losses.

However, all this investment trading is still more an art than a science, despite the scientific pretensions of many of its practitioners. This was the view of Edward C. Johnson Jr, considered by many to be the dean of Wall Street, who after 60 years of experience in the markets remarked:

"I have been absorbed and immersed since 1924 in the market and I know this is no science. It is an art form...it is personal intuition, sensing patterns of behaviour. The market is like a beautiful woman — endlessly fascinating, endlessly complex, always changing, always mystifying."

Bibliography

Band, Richard E., "Contrary Investing for the 90s" (Investment Library, Melbourne, 1989)

Bannock, Graham, **Baxter**, R.E. and **Rees**, Ray. "The Penguin Dictionary of Economics" (Penguin Books, England, 1971)

Browne, Harry. "Why the Best-Laid Investment Plans Usually go Wrong" (Fireside, New York, 1989)

Chia, Robert and **Soh**, Doreen. "How to Invest in Stocks and Shares" (Times Books International, Singapore, 4th edition, 1993)

Cheong, Sally. "Investing in Unit Trusts in Malaysia" (Corporate Research Services Sdn Bhd, Kuala Lumpur, 1994)

Dreman, David N. "Psychology and the Stock Market" (AMACOM, New York, 1977)

Financial Planner. "Directory of Personal Investments 1997" (Ins Publications Pte Ltd, Singapore, 1995)

Goh, Kheng Chuan. "Handbook for Stock Investors" (Rank Books, Singapore, 1993)

Goodspeed, Bennett W. "The Tao Jones Averages" (Penguin Books, New York, 1983)

Gunther, Max. "The Zurich Axioms"
(Unwin Paperbacks, London, 1985)

Leeb, Stephen. "Market Timing for the Nineties"
(HarperBusiness, New York, 1993)

Low, Buen Sin and **Lye** Chiew Meng. "Stock Options"
(EPB Publishers, Singapore, 1994)

Malkiel, Burton G. "A Random Walk Down Wall Street"
(W. W. Norton and Co, New York, 1990)

Miller, Lowell. "The Perfect Investment"
(E.P. Dutton, New York, 1983)

McCafferty, Thomas and **Wasendorf**, Russell. "All About
Futures" (Golden Books Centre Sdn Bhd, Kuala Lumpur,
1992)

Sarnoff, Paul. "Trading in Gold"
(Woodhead Faulkner, London, 1989)

Saw, Swee-Hock, "Investment Management"
(Longman Singapore and the Stock Exchange of Singapore,
2nd edition, 1991)

Slayter, Will and **Carew**, Edna. "Trading Asia-Pacific Financial
Futures Markets" (Allen and Unwin, Australia, 1993)

Smith, Adam (pseudonym). "The Money Game"
(Michael Joseph, London, 1968)

Soh, Doreen. "How to Invest in Commodities, Gold & Currencies"(Times Books International, Singapore, 1994)

Tan, Chwee Huat. "Financial Markets and Institutions in Singapore" (Singapore University Press, Singapore, 7th edition, 1992)

Tay, Swee Kian (Catherine) "Investing in Stocks and Shares" (Specialist Press, Singapore, 2nd edition, 1995)

Wong Yee. "A Guide to Investment in Stocks and Shares" (EPB Publishers, Singapore, 3rd edition, 1991)

Wong Yee. "Practical Knowledge in Shares Investment" (EPB Publishers, Singapore, 1993)

Index